ILLUSTRATED GUIDE TO ROSES

Illustrated
Guide to Roses

by FRED FAIRBROTHER, MSc, FRIC

PEARSON · LONDON

Printed in Great Britain by Jarrold & Sons Ltd, Norwich
for C. Arthur Pearson Limited, Southampton Street, London W.C.2

Contents

AUTHOR'S ACKNOWLEDGEMENTS

My grateful thanks for the loan of the colour transparencies reproduced in this book are due to Dr A. Dick, Alex. Dickson & Sons, C. W. Gregory & Son, Sam McGredy & Son, The Royal National Rose Society, and John Sanday (Roses) Ltd.

I am also greatly indebted to *Amateur Gardening*, A. Cook, Esq., Alex. Dickson & Sons, J. E. Downward, FIBP, C. W. Gregory & Son Ltd, A. J. Huxley, Esq., Sam McGredy & Son, Miss Elsa M. Megson, H. Smith, Esq. and Wheatcroft Brothers for permission to reproduce their black-and-white photographs in this book.

I should also like to thank my publishers for their helpful suggestions at all times during the production of this book.

Introduction

In compiling Pearson's *Illustrated Guide to Roses*, as well as discussing the more usual preparation of soil and subsequent treatment of the planted trees, I have given a full description of pruning the different types of trees and dealt at length with ramblers and climbers. There are special chapters dealing with miniature roses, roses suitable for indoor decoration and roses for the beginner, so that the amateur can pick out quickly those varieties which he may wish to grow for a specific purpose.

Chaplin's Pink Climber

Few flowers are easier to grow than roses and none gives greater return of beautiful blooms for the labour expended. As is explained later, this labour must be given but the results are most rewarding. The garden roses are in bloom from June to November, almost six months of riotous colour and fragrance. What other flower can equal this? Also for beauty and variety of form what flower can surpass this Queen of Flowers, the Rose?

The genus *Rosa* also provides a variety of types which can be used for various purposes in the garden, whether it be for richly coloured and fragrant beds, or for fences providing beauty as well as protection, or for covering unsightly spots in the garden or for growing on walls, pergolas or poles. With such a variety of uses it is not surprising that the rose garden, however small, makes its intense appeal to so many flower-lovers.

F. F.

I. Suitability of Soil

Although the rose is very tolerant and will grow in a variety of soils, it is capable of producing better results in certain types of soils than in others. Soils vary in texture from sandy soils to clay soils and from acid peaty soils to alkaline chalky soils.

Sandy soils consist of large particles (coarse sand 2·00–0·20 mm. in diameter, fine sand 0·20–0·02 mm. in diameter) and consequently have large pore spaces, i.e. the space between individual particles. This enables water and solutions of plant food to pass through them all too easily.

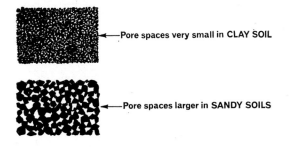

—Pore spaces very small in CLAY SOIL

—Pore spaces larger in SANDY SOILS

Clay on the other hand consists of extremely small particles (less than 0·002 mm. in diameter) and the small pore spaces between these particles hold water and food solutions very tenaciously. Unless well drained, such soils tend to become waterlogged and cold, conditions not conducive to good growth. And yet, with thorough cultivation, they can be converted into most fertile soils.

Somewhere between these two extremes in size of particles is *silt* which is often carried down by rivers and deposited on the land during flooding. A mixture of sand, silt and clay is called *loam* and the soil may be classed as a sandy loam, a silt loam or a clay loam, according to the proportion of the kind of particles it contains. A clay loam is excellently suitable as a basic soil for roses. The right kind of texture can be roughly judged by compressing a handful of moist soil, then if it crumbles when the hand is opened and the soil touched with a finger one can be fairly certain the soil is of the right *texture*.

For a fertile soil, however, there is still something lacking. For the successful culture of roses the soil must contain that most important substance, *humus*. Humus is the final product of the decomposition of organic matter. This decomposition is brought about by numerous bacteria, micro-organisms which use the carbon of the organic matter for their own energy and when the conditions of temperature are satisfactory they break down the organic matter into soluble salts suitable for feeding the trees. The organic content of a soil can be increased by the addition of farmyard manure, home-made compost or composted horse manure. Even old newspapers or cast-off woollen clothing cut into strips can be used to improve the nature of the subsoil. Spent hops and peat are excellent substances to add to any type of soil. They both provide humus which is invaluable to the rose grower. Humus has great water-holding properties and so will help a sandy soil to retain its moisture and not dry out so quickly. Also it has the power of coagulating the fine particles of a clay soil into groups thus increasing the *individual* size of the pore spaces and thereby giving greater aeration and better facility for drainage. Humus therefore will make sandy loams capable of retaining water and at the same time it helps to make clay more porous. *Gypsum*, natural calcium sulphate, added at the rate of 4–8 oz. per square yard also has the power of coagulating the particles of clay and thus making its texture more crumbly and less sticky.

Ridging the bed and leaving the rough ridges to weather in the winter will help to break up a clay soil.

A ridged rose bed

Gravelly soils require the addition of generous quantities of bulky organic matter, e.g. compost, manure, spent hops (or hop manure) and these should be mixed into the topsoil and not buried in the subsoil where they might easily be lost before the plant can make use of them, and before there is any chance to retain water and food solutions.

Chalky soils are difficult for the rose-grower, as they are generally alkaline, though some may be neutral. Roses grow best on a slightly acid soil and the chalky soils tend to cause chlorosis (a yellowing of the leaves due to a lack of chlorophyll). Such soils can be improved by the addition of organic manures, or by growing a crop of mustard on the land and digging the green plants into the top 6–9 ins. The addition of green sulphur 2–4 oz. per square yard will tend to reduce the alkalinity. Also, during the growing season, treating the trees with Sequestrene Plus lessens the incidence of chlorosis.

The acidity and alkalinity of a soil are indicated on a scale known as the pH (potential of hydrogen) scale. It ranges from 1 to 14, 1 being *very* strongly acid and 14 *very* strongly alkaline while a soil of 7 is neutral. Roses grow best in a soil with a pH 6·0 to 6·5. It is not necessary for the practical gardener to know how such a scale has been compiled; all he needs is a method by which he can roughly determine the pH value. This can be done by using strips of paper* containing indicators which change colour at certain points on the scale or between closely associated points. The method used is to stir some soil with boiled rainwater which has been subsequently cooled. This can be done quite efficiently in a saucer or cup. The paper is dipped in and then rinsed with some of the clean boiled rainwater and the change noted. The pH value corresponding to the colour change is indicated on the packet of strips, which can be obtained from a horticultural sundries salesman. A pocket set of soil-testing reagents is made up by British Drug Houses and sold by chemists. Full instructions for use are given with the set. You can also test the soil for its various nutrient salts content with a Sudbury soil-testing outfit (obtainable through horticultural shops).

2. Preparation of Rose Beds

Happy is the man who has a depth of 18 ins. to 2 ft. of good soil in his garden; he can apply the orthodox method of double-digging with ease as he is not worried by the nature of the subsoil. If, however, there is only 6 ins. of topsoil above clay or chalk it is no use talking about 'taking out the top spit', i.e. the length of a spade blade (about 9–10 ins.) because it simply isn't there. In such cases the term 'top spit' should be interpreted as topsoil, however shallow this may be.

Double-Digging

Mark out a strip 18 ins. wide across the width of the bed, at one end. Dig out the topsoil, if possible to a depth of 9–10 ins. and wheel it to the opposite end of the bed. Dig a clean trench, removing the crumbs of topsoil but not taking any of the subsoil. The latter can usually be detected by its different colour and texture. Break up the subsoil to a depth of 9–10 ins. using a pick if necessary, but it *must* be broken up. Then spread on the surface a generous supply of manure or compost enriched with a good handful of superphosphate per square yard of trench. If the bed is 6 ft. wide and the trench 18 ins. wide this means one good handful per trench. Dig this manure into the broken subsoil. Next move the line marking the first trench 18 ins. along the bed, dig out the topsoil to the same depth as before and transfer it into the first trench, working backwards and transferring the soil sideways. This enables you to keep a clean trench of the correct width. Break up the subsoil of this second trench and treat it in the same way as the first trench. Continue to the end of the bed, the length of which should be some multiple of 1 ft. 6 ins. (e.g. 9 ft., 12 ft., 18 ft., etc.), filling in the last trench with the soil taken from the first trench *A*.

If done carefully the bed should now be quite level and it should be left for several weeks to

* These papers can be obtained from Pan Britannica Industries Ltd, Waltham Cross, Herts.

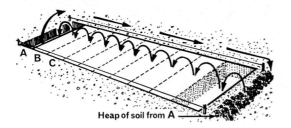

Heap of soil from A

settle before planting. This is to eliminate air pockets which prevent the root hairs coming into contact with the food solutions in the soil. As planting may begin in mid-November or even in October, it is well to prepare the new rose bed at the end of August or early in September.

If the bed is a wide one, say, 10–15 ft., put a line down the centre running from one end of the bed to the other. The diagram below shows how the work should proceed; the method of preparation of the bed remains the same.

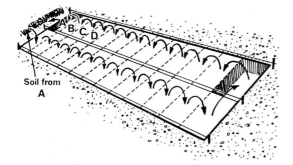

Soil from A

3. Selecting New Rose Trees and Treatment when they Arrive

Before deciding what varieties to buy, try to visit a good rose nursery, or visit the display gardens in the public parks or the Royal National Rose Society's display garden at St Albans, Hertfordshire. You will then see how the different varieties grow when given reasonable attention. Take particular note of the height, width and planting distances of the different varieties. This you cannot get from catalogues, fascinating though they are, nor from the displays at shows where attention is focused on the blooms alone.

It certainly pays to take the trouble to visit a good nursery after you have made your preliminary catalogue selection. In making your selection for inspection, the list starting on page 48 should be a help to you.

When you have ordered the trees—and it is a wise precaution to order early—you can concentrate on the preparation of suitable beds to receive them, as they will not arrive before November.

They are carefully packed by the nurserymen, either in sacking, the roots being protected by moist straw; in polythene bags; or in containers filled with soil, and can be allowed to remain a week or so in a shed or garage if it is not convenient to unpack them immediately. If the weather is frosty or if for any reason the soil in the beds is not in a fit condition for planting, carefully unpack the trees, cut off any leaves left on the stems—do

not tear them off—also shorten the stems just below any flower buds. Trim off any bruised roots and shorten any long ropy ones.

As a precaution against the possibility of fungoid diseases, e.g. Black Spot, Rust, Mildew, being dormant on the stems and roots, it is wise to immerse the trees completely in a solution of permanganate of potash, 1 oz./4 gallons or Condy's Fluid, 2 tablespoonfuls to a gallon of water.

'Heeling in' rose trees

Immersing tree roots as a protection against diseases

Having taken these precautions bury the roots and one quarter of the length of the stems in a trench dug in some spare ground in the garden. This is called 'heeling in'. The trees should be 'heeled in' separately, the soil being finally pressed down over the roots. The trees can remain in this position for several months if planting conditions are unfavourable, but planting should be completed by the end of March or early April. It is advisable to make a plan showing the position of each variety as labels have a habit of rotting or being blown off.

Planting

The rose trees may be planted any time from November to the end of March, provided the soil is free from frost and not too wet. As suitable days are somewhat rare in the winter months, everything should be ready for use when such a day arrives.

Have a planting mixture of 1 pailful of loam, 1 pailful of peat, and 2 handfuls of bonemeal kept just moist and ready for use. Keep it under cover and turn it occasionally to ensure thorough mixing.

A hole sufficiently large to take the roots spread out is dug where the tree is to be planted. If the roots on the trees from the nursery are more or less symmetrically arranged round the stem they can be arranged to fall down the sides of a mound of the planting mixture placed in the middle of the base of the hole. More planting mixture is then worked round the roots and the soil which was dug out to make the hole is finally filled into the hole and pressed firmly round the tree, the junction of the tree and the root-stock being 1 in. below the final surface of the soil. Don't overdo the firming, remember you are planting a living tree and not a wooden post. The firming is to eliminate any large air cavities in the soil and also to lessen the tendency to rocking and twisting in the wind before the roots have established themselves.

Unfortunately trees do not usually arrive with

their roots so conveniently arranged. They are more generally growing in one direction and they resist being forced into a circular position. The best plan is to plant the tree so that the roots will grow in the pattern already established. To accommodate the roots of such trees it is convenient to dig a rectangular hole 1 ft. by 1½ ft. with a sloping base and about 3 ins. deep at the shallow end and 9 ins. at the deep end. Cover the base of the hole with about 1 in. of the prepared planting mixture. The roots are then spread evenly and downwards along the sloping base and the junction of the tree with the root stock should be 1 in. below the surface of the soil when the hole is filled in and the soil pressed firmly over the roots. More planting mixture should be used to cover the roots at least 1 in. and it should be worked between the roots with the fingers. The hole is then filled in with the soil originally dug out. If the planting is done in March the trees may be pruned before planting. Trees planted in the autumn need not be pruned until the following March but the stems should be shortened a little so as to offer less wind resistance.

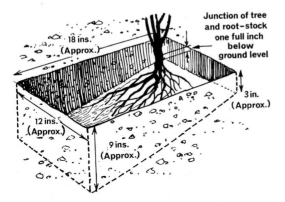

If a dead tree is being replaced in an established bed, the soil should be dug out to a depth of 12 ins. and as wide and broad as the space between the other trees allows. The hole should be filled with soil from some part of the garden where roses have not been grown for some time. The reason for this is that the soil round the dead tree may be diseased or lacking in food and humus. The new soil should be enriched by the addition of some old chopped manure or failing this by the

planting mixture already referred to, to which has been added a handful of rose fertiliser. The new tree can then be planted in the way described above.

When planting standards, proceed in the same way as for bushes but before filling in the soil drive a good stake into the ground near the stem of the standard avoiding damaging the roots. The stake should be high enough to reach just below the head of the standard and the tree then tied temporarily to the stake. After a few days untie the tree, press the roots down again in case there has been any further settling of the soil and then re-tie the standard to the stake using either rubber or strips of sacking wrapped round the stem before tying to prevent any possible chafing.

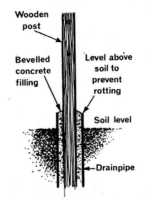

Climbers and ramblers should be planted 9 ins. to 1 ft. away from the support to which they will be secured and the stems trained on short canes to reach the support. If the climbing roses are required to be trained as a screen a good method is to secure the stems to covered wires stretched between posts. These posts should either be made of concrete or of larch or pine which has been soaked in creosote, after removing the bark, some weeks before being used, and the part in the ground encased by a drainpipe, the space between the pipe and the post being filled with concrete. (These precautions will prolong the life of the wooden posts.) The posts should be set in line about 12 ft. apart and bored for the eye-bolts at regular intervals up the posts. The wires should be stretched taut at intervals of 10 ins. to 12 ins. to allow the stems to be trained fairly horizontally.

An attractive way of training climbers and ramblers is to build a tripod of long concrete posts and arrange wires round them at intervals of 1 ft. Plant the rose trees *between* the posts and train them on the wires, thus giving a solid pyramid of roses in summer.

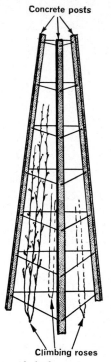

The spacing of different types of roses when planting depends on the vigour of the particular variety. Generally, the hybrid teas can be planted 1 ft. 9 ins. apart but strong growing varieties, e.g. Peace, Eden Rose, Pink Favourite, Red Ensign, should be spaced 2 ft. 6 ins. apart. Floribundas may be planted 2 ft. apart and shrub roses 3–4 ft. apart. Climbers or ramblers trained on fences should be planted 6–8 ft. apart.

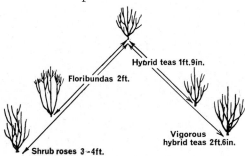

4. Pruning of the Different Types

It is curious how this comparatively simple operation puzzles so many rose-growers, and not only the beginners. Probably the reason is the multiplicity of advice from the experts who rarely agree as to time for pruning and whether pruning should be severe, moderate or light.

Why is pruning necessary? Simply (*a*) to keep the tree within reasonable bounds, (*b*) to remove dead and useless, thin, twiggy growths, and (*c*) to let air and light into the tree.

What is the best season for pruning? Any time after the leaves have fallen, i.e. from the end of November to the time when the new leaf-buds begin to fatten preliminary to bursting into leaf: i.e. early March or April, depending on whether you live in a mild or severe climate. This does not apply to ramblers, which are pruned in October after the summer flowering is over. It is unwise to prune during a hard frost, but provided the operations are completed in a mild spell subsequent frost will do no harm until after the tree has started to grow. This growth will not occur in any case until early spring though a mild February has been known to develop early growth and this is dangerous. A frost in May is the really damaging frost and this is just as disastrous whether the trees are pruned in March or in November. I find the trees bloom earlier if pruned in November, as the dormant buds have a longer period in which to fatten up and when growth actually starts, it goes quickly to maturity. The probable reason for so many rosarians advocating pruning in mid-March is that they have in mind the 'Show' date early in July.

Their pruning date is governed by the date of the Show. For garden display this does not matter and after all, the weather has the final say for the best laid schemes o' mice an' men gang aft a-gley.

Pruning of various types

(a) *Hybrid teas*. The simplest of all pruning is that of the 'maiden' tree received from the nurseryman. It has no dead wood, few or no twiggy growths

Remove thin, weak growths cleanly from the base

Maiden tree as planted

and from three to six stems all growing from the base. These maiden trees have flowered in the nursery, for the first time, during the summer prior to your purchasing them in November. Sometimes the trees arrive with their stems shortened, but do not be tempted to think that they have been pruned. This shortening is largely to facilitate packing and lessen the charges for transport. Such trees should be planted as early as possible after arrival, always assuming the conditions of soil and weather are favourable, and the pruning may be left until March or they can be pruned before planting, thus avoiding a double dose of stooping—a consideration as one gets older! On all soils except very poor or sandy ones, pruning should be severe during the first year.

Cut back each main shoot to just above a bud, leaving two or three buds on the remaining part of the shoot (i.e. 4–6 ins. long)

The trees should be cut back to not more than 4 ins.–6 ins. from the point where the tree is joined to the stock. On sandy soils it is better to prune moderately, i.e. 9 ins. above the junction with the root-stock, and then prune more severely in the second year. There are some exceptions to the above general rules, e.g. yellow roses do not respond well to severe pruning and a few others, e.g. Bacchus, Peace, Eden Rose do better with moderate pruning. Such exceptions can only be discovered by experience as conditions of soil and climate are factors to be reckoned with.

Pruning of maiden tree completed. Each shoot is cut back to an outward pointing bud

The older trees, say 3 to 5 years old, present a distinctly different picture from the maiden trees. Here there are many stems to be dealt with, some crossing over other stems, others growing towards the centre of the tree, many poor, twiggy growths and a certain amount of dead wood. So as to avoid too much labour at a given time it is advisable to do some preliminary work during the winter months. All dead wood can be cut down to the base. Later the stems growing in bad positions can be removed and finally the remaining stems shortened to the required length, i.e. about 6 ins. above the ground-level. Finally the pruned, old tree should be examined for 'stubs' which are old and useless and these should be removed either

with the pruning saw or sharp secateurs. Before leaving the tree, take a final look at it to see if more older woody stubs can be removed with advantage. A study of the illustrations will help the beginner to deal with these older trees.

An older hybrid tea or floribunda bush before pruning

Remove thin, weak shoots to leave the main strong-growing branches. Cut away all dead wood cleanly

Prune back the main branches to a half or a third of their present growth. The extent of the pruning must depend on the variety and condition of the bush. As a general rule though, a neglected bush should be pruned severely, as illustrated here

Pruning completed. This type of pruning is of benefit on an old bush, encouraging strong new growth from the base

(b) *Floribundas*. These may be pruned in the same way as the hybrid teas but somewhat less severely. Floribundas are generally much stronger-growing trees and present problems similar to those of the old hybrid teas but at a much earlier age. It is only during the first two years that the pruning of floribundas is really easy. The method adopted with these is similar to that used on a young hybrid tea. First remove any weak or dead wood so as to get a main framework for pruning. Then shorten the stems to about 9 ins. above ground.

For established, e.g. 3- to 5-year-old trees, the illustrations showing the steps in the pruning of old hybrid teas should be followed.

When pruning is nearly completed take a final look at the tree. Check whether any woody stubs, which are old and useless, can be removed with advantage, such as the one to the right of this bush, with sharp secateurs or a pruning saw

When pruning a young floribunda first take out weak and dead wood shoots, cutting out the wood cleanly from the base or point of origin

Young floribunda framework branches ready for pruning

Pruning of floribunda completed

Cut branches back to about half-way or slightly less if the bush is very strong, slightly more if weak growing. Cut to an outward pointing bud

If a tree has been neglected for a few years and is beginning to assume shrub proportions, it might be too much of a shock to the tree to prune drastically all the stems. In such cases select about half the stems from different parts of the tree and prune these severely, leaving the other half lightly pruned until the following year.

(c) *Shrubs.* These can only be grown successfully in fairly large gardens, as each variety requires considerable space. They require little pruning; all dead and useless wood should be cut away and a few of the very long stems shortened to keep them within bounds. This must not be overdone as many shrubs give their best blooms at the tips of the branches. If dead flower-heads are removed, the long stems often throw out side shoots which may flower again in the autumn and certainly will provide short flowering stems for next year. A good example of this type of shrub is the R. *rugosa* hybrid Roseraie de l'Hay. Treated in the above way it will produce, when fully matured, hundreds of blooms during the season. It will reach a height of 8 ft. and has a spread of nearly as much. A hedge of it is a joy to those who like deep purplish crimson blooms. It is sweetly fragrant. Many of the shrub roses will make good hedges and lend colour to the garden at the same time.

(d) *Standard Roses.* The ordinary upright-growing standard which is a hybrid tea or a floribunda budded 4 or 5 ft. above ground-level is pruned exactly as the bushes of the same variety but the pruning should not be quite so severe. Care should be taken to cut out badly placed stems and the stems should be pruned to 'eyes' pointing towards a vacant place. This will help to produce a symmetrically shaped head. Standard roses of full height should not be planted in a very exposed windy position, as there is a danger of the head being blown out even if the tree is well staked. It is far better to use half or quarter standards in such positions.

Pruning of standard completed. This type of pruning aims at keeping the centre of the head open, and an outward pointing branch formation. This gives balanced growth and a well-shaped head

When pruning standard roses follow the same principles as a bush rose, first taking out any thin twiggy or crossing shoots. These should be removed flush with the branch from which they arise

After the thin twiggy growths and the crossing shoots have been removed, shorten back the main branches to about half-way, always cutting to an outward pointing bud

(e) *Weeping Standards*. These certainly require a sheltered position. They are popular as specimen trees in lawns and rambler roses give the best types. These standards are usually budded on a long stem, 6 or 7 ft. above ground-level, and varieties such as Excelsa, Crimson Shower, Dorothy Perkins, Mary Wallace, which have a natural trailing habit,

produce better specimens than the more upright-growing climbers. The pruning consists of cutting away completely any thin twiggy growths from the centre of the head and shortening fairly severely stems which have flowered. The long new stems which grow during the flowering season must be carefully preserved and not shortened at all. It is wise to secure them to canes arranged symmetrically round the tree so as to provide a shapely weeping standard full of bloom the following season. The more strong growths you can encourage the more stems which have carried blooms can be cut hard back. Then new ones released from the canes can take their place.

(f) *Ramblers and Climbers*. These two classes seem to present the greatest difficulty with regard to pruning. This is because they do not fall into a general pattern. Some of the ramblers throw long new stems from the base each year; these will be classed 'A'. Such are easy to prune; just cut away from the base all the old wood that has flowered during the summer and tie-in the new stems. This should be done in September or October. Other ramblers, class 'B', develop few new stems from the base but good strong longish shoots grow out of the old wood some distance up the stem. When pruning, cut back the old stems which have flowered to a point just above the strongest of the side shoots and tie these new shoots into position. If there are shorter growths below the long ones shorten them to two or three eyes from the main stem. Again, this pruning should be done in September or October after flowering.

Ramblers

Class A

Crimson Rambler
Crimson Shower
Dorothy Perkins
Excelsa

François Juranville
Mary Wallace
Minnehaha
Sanders' White

Class B

Albéric Barbier
Albertine
American Pillar
Blaze
Chaplin's Pink
Chaplin's Pink
  Companion
Crimson Conquest

Dr Van Fleet
Easlea's Golden
  Rambler
Emily Gray
New Dawn
Paul's Scarlet Climber
Veilchenblau

The climbers also fall into two classes, 'C' and 'D'. To class C belong the climbing sports of the hybrid teas and one or two of the large flowering climbers. These are pruned in winter or early spring. No new growths should be pruned unless they are damaged and then as much as possible is retained. Old or worn-out wood should be cut out and laterals on the newer wood cut back to a few eyes from where they started, the weaker ones being pruned the hardest. Also, as these climbers tend to grow leggy and produce their blooms high up on the stems, train them as near the horizontal as possible. To class D belong the moderate climbers or pillar roses, many of the large flowering climbers, and any climbing floribundas. These require little or no pruning, just the removal of dead, old and worn-out wood and shortening of some of the longer stems to keep the tree in good shape. They should not be pruned at all in the first year.

Climbers

Class C

Cl. Crimson Glory
Cl. Ena Harkness

Cl. Etoile de Hollande
Cl. Golden Dawn

Cl. Lady Hillingdon
Cl. Lady Sylvia
Cl. Mme Butterfly
Cl. Mme Caroline
  Testout
Cl. Mme Henri
  Guillot
Cl. Mrs Sam McGredy

Cl. Mme Edouard
  Herriot
Cl. Ophelia
Cl. Peace
Cl. Shot Silk
Mme Grégoire
  Staechelin

Class D

Allen Chandler
Aloha
Casino★
Clair Matin★
Copenhagen★
Coral Dawn
Cupid
Danse du Feu
Danse des Sylphes
Dortmund
Etude
Elegance
Golden Glow
Golden Showers
Cl. Goldilocks
Guinée
Hamburger Phoenix
Joseph's Coat★
Kathleen Harrop

Cl. Korona
Leverküsen
Maigold
Cl. Masquerade
Meg
Norwich Pink
Norwich Salmon
Parade
Paul's Lemon Pillar
Phyllis Bide
Pink Cloud
Pink Perpetue
Raymond Chenault
Ritter von Barmstede
Royal Gold
Soldier Boy
High Noon
Zéphirine Drouhin
Zweibrücken

In all types the pruning cut should be made just above an 'eye' (leaf-bud), see illustration below.

★ Semi Climber.

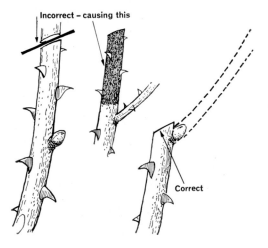

Incorrect – causing this

Correct

5. The Feeding of Rose Trees

Rose trees, in common with other green-leaved trees, are capable of building up much of their food by a process known as photosynthesis. This is carried out in the leaves where the energy of the sun is used to join together two chemical substances, carbon dioxide and water, thus forming carbohydrates in the form of sugars, starches and cellulose, at the same time liberating oxygen. The carbon dioxide is taken from the air through the leaves as is some of the water but the main source of water is the soil from which it is extracted by the root hairs. In order to bring about this chemical reaction a green substance, chlorophyll, which is built up in the leaves in presence of sunlight, is essential. Chlorophyll is a very complex substance chemically, the molecule containing carbon, hydrogen, oxygen, nitrogen and magnesium atoms. Iron and probably manganese play an important part as catalysts, helping to form the molecule but not actually being part of it. If iron is not available in the soil the chlorophyll molecule cannot be built up and the leaves begin to turn yellow, signifying that chlorosis has set in. Magnesium must also be available as it is actually present in the chlorophyll molecule and absence of it will also cause chlorosis, the leaves showing yellow or purple discoloration between the main veins of the leaves. Thus it is obvious that the soil must contain soluble salts of iron and magnesium.

Other essential elements required as soluble salts are potassium, phosphorus and nitrogen. The potassium is usually supplied as potassium sulphate or potassium nitrate, the latter also providing some nitrogen; the phosphorus is supplied as phosphates, bonemeal or superphosphate of calcium being the usual types; nitrogen, as well as being supplied by potassium nitrate, may be supplied by sulphate of ammonia. Soils vary in chemical composition as well as texture and it is advisable to have your soil tested before you begin to treat it with chemical fertilisers. More damage is probably done by well-meaning beginners who overfeed their rose trees than by any other cause. If the rose bed has been properly prepared and well manured, there is no need to add extra manure during the first year after planting, except that in September a treatment of the beds with sulphate of potash, 2 oz. per square yard, will help to harden the stems before winter. A good mulch of moist peat or leaf-mould covering the beds 1½ ins. thick will do more good by conserving moisture in the soil during the first year than will extra manure or fertilisers. On no account must these young trees be allowed to become too dry.

Mulching a rose tree

It may be necessary as the summer advances to treat any trees which show any sign of chlorosis with 1 oz. of Epsom salts (magnesium sulphate) per square yard of surface soil and water it in, or make a solution of 1 oz. Epsom salts per gallon of water and apply, through the rose of a watering-can, 1 gallon per square yard of surface soil.

After the first year it will be necessary to replenish the food supply in the beds and the first treatment should be given in early spring after pruning. If good farmyard manure can be obtained I consider there is nothing to beat it. A good dressing 2 ins. thick of finely chopped manure, that has been stacked covered during the winter, hoed into the surface soil is excellent. Unfortunately, such manure is not always easy to come by, especially by town-dwellers, but composted horse manure is available from horticultural suppliers in quantities suitable for small gardens. If you have sufficient vegetable waste to make a good compost heap, this can be used as a mulch. Peat has no food value, but if a good rose fertiliser is spread over the soil at the rate recommended by the makers and lightly hoed in before the peat is put on, the results should be good.

If you wish to make up your own fertiliser, the following is a good general formula:

2 parts by weight of potassium nitrate
1 part by weight of sulphate of ammonia
5 parts by weight of calcium superphosphate (superphosphate of lime)
2 parts by weight of sulphate of potash
1 part by weight of commercial magnesium sulphate (Epsom salts)
1 part by weight ferrous sulphate (green sulphate of iron)

Thorough mixing of the ingredients is very important. The mixture should be sprinkled evenly over the surface soil at the rate of 2 oz. per square yard given twice at an interval of two or three weeks. (A normal handful is about 4 oz.)

No further feeding is necessary until the first flowering is over and all dead heads removed. These should be cut off with secateurs to a good out-pointing eye below the flower-head. At the same time any suckers which are growing from the base of the tree should be removed. They can be recognised by the different colour and texture of the leaves and stems. If they are not removed they will weaken and in time kill the trees. They should be pulled out from the stem or cut very close to the point of origin even if this means removing a little soil from the base to find this point. It is useless to cut them off at soil-level as they will then produce several suckers from the eyes left in the part below the soil. When all this has been done give the beds one more dressing of the fertiliser, this time applying 3 oz. per square

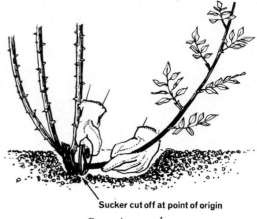

Sucker cut off at point of origin

Removing a sucker

yard and hoeing it in. If the weather is dry the beds should be watered.

It is advisable to vary the type of food the following year by applying in place of the inorganic fertiliser a mixture of equal parts of fish manure and powdered hoof and horn or meat and bonemeal. Remember it is a golden rule not to overdo the feeding and never try to revive a weak tree by giving an extra dose of fertiliser. It is far better to water it and if it doesn't respond, dig it up in the autumn and examine the roots for disease. It may be that changing the soil in which the tree has grown will revive it, or it may be advisable to scrap the tree and buy another variety for that spot.

6. Spring and Summer Care

In order to have first-class blooms during the late spring and early summer it is essential to have healthy trees with good clean foliage throughout the growing season. Roses, in common with all living things, are subject to attacks from certain pests which feed or prey upon them, and are also subject to a few troublesome diseases against which preventive action must be taken. There is no doubt that good cultivation deters many of these troubles, for plants which have their roots water-logged and which are subjected to badly balanced diet will never thrive. In certain areas and under certain climatic conditions, even if the greatest care has been taken with cultivation, it is impossible to go through a rose season without one or more troublesome pests or illnesses. Of the pests, greenfly, caterpillars, thrips are the commonest, but sometimes the leaf-cutting bee, the leaf-rolling sawfly and the chafer beetles can cause trouble.

Greenfly, aphis, is about the earliest of the troubles but it can easily be controlled if sprayed in time. There are many insecticides which can be effectively applied and the newer systemic ones are effective over a fairly long period. Spray thoroughly under and over the leaves and particularly the tips of the stems where the flower-buds are forming. Other general rules relating to spraying are: always keep strictly to the strength of solution indicated on the container, also do not spray in hot sun or scorching of the leaves is sure to occur. Spray as soon as the first greenflies appear and then spray again if and when they make a reappearance. Usually two sprayings applied at the right time will take care of this pest. Greenflies are so called because green is their usual colour, but they may be pink or brown. They are sucking insects and feed on the juices of young leaves and buds. Look out for the long thin grey grubs with a dark stripe

along the back. These are the larvae of the ladybirds and as they feed on the greenfly they are your best allies and should never be destroyed.

Rose affected by caterpillars of the rose tortrix moth

Caterpillars of the rose tortrix moth. There are two varieties of this pest, one is green and wriggles about, the other is fatter and brown and is sluggish in movement. The former attacks the young leaves and the latter usually attacks the young flower-buds. These caterpillars can do considerable damage unless destroyed early. By day both of these conceal themselves by curling inside young leaves near the flower-buds and at night they emerge to feed on these leaves. Suspect any closed-up leaves, or even two leaves stuck together. The best method of dealing with these pests is to pick them off by hand either by unfolding the leaves, which is troublesome, or by removing the curled leaves and killing the grubs by squeezing the leaves. DDT powder has been suggested but this is harmful to the larvae of the ladybirds and should be avoided.

Thrips are minute four-winged flies less than

Rose attacked by greenfly

$\frac{1}{20}$ in. long which attack the roses just as the buds are opening. They give the edges of the petals of the opening roses a burnt appearance and the full flower is often malformed. A dry spring is very conducive to attacks by this pest and certain varieties, particularly those of the Ophelia group—Mme Butterfly, Lady Sylvia and certain of the yellows. Diptrex or Pyrethrex powder carefully dusted on the buds just as they are opening is most effective. Occasionally the rose leaves are attacked by the *leaf-cutting bees*. These ingenious insects cut circular or semicircular pieces out of the leaves with geometrical exactness and carry them off to line their nests which are usually found in banks of dry earth. The only way to deal with this pest is to watch the bees in the evening when they return to their nests and destroy them.

Rose attacked by thrips fly

Chafer beetles and their grubs. Three varieties attack roses: the cockchafer, the garden chafer and the rose chafer. They are often to be seen in May and June and they attack the foliage, buds and flowers. Occasionally one finds a rose bloom half of which is chafed away as though by the thorns of a neighbouring stem. Much damage is also done to the roots near which the larvae are feeding. The larvae of all the chafers are similar in appearance. They are a dirty white colour about 1 in. to $1\frac{1}{2}$ ins. long and can be seen in the soil when digging in preparation of the beds. This is the best time to destroy them. They are very sluggish in their movements and can easily be caught and destroyed. Once they are established in the soil it is difficult to eradicate them. A good countermeasure is the application to the soil of Gam-

mexane (benzene hexachloride) in early June as this repels the egg-laying chafers. For the destruction of very young garden and rose chafers add Pyrethrex to DDT emulsion and spray. The spray is ineffective on the adult chafers.

The leaf-rolling sawfly. The larvae of the black shining sawflies are pale green or whitish and are laid in May or early June on the young leaves. They roll themselves in the leaves (which disfigures the foliage) and rob the tree of the food which the leaves should provide by feeding on the rolled leaves. The rolled leaves should be removed and burnt early in the season, thus preventing a further supply of sawflies the following year. An effective control is provided by spraying the trees with DDT plus Pyrethrex in late April when the flies may be seen hovering over the trees.

Fortunately for the rose-grower, not all these pests appear in all places nor in all seasons, but they can occasionally be troublesome and should be dealt with promptly. The principal illnesses to which rose trees are prone are (*a*) those caused by some soil deficiency or an excess of some chemical element, e.g. *chlorosis, purple spotting, purple markings between the veins in the leaves*, and (*b*) those which are caused by some fungus or spores, e.g. *Mildew, Black Spot, Rust.*

Rose leaves affected by the leaf-rolling sawfly

Chlorosis is easily observed by the yellowing of the leaves. Sometimes late in the season an otherwise healthy tree with rich green foliage will have some leaves at the base of the tree which turn yellow. Don't worry too much about these—just remove them. It is when many of the leaves higher up the stems of the trees become yellowish that the protective measures mentioned below should be taken.

The appearance of chlorosis does not necessarily indicate a shortage of iron in the soil, it merely tells you that the iron is not available to the plants. Where the soil has a high pH or contains an excess of lime or chalk or phosphates, salts of hydroxide, carbonate or phosphate of iron are formed and these salts being insoluble cannot be absorbed by the rose trees. Substances known as sequestrenes, for the prevention and treatment of chlorosis in trees growing on such types of soil, can be bought. The sequestrenes are complex organic acids which contain iron in a 'bound' condition. This iron does not form insoluble salts in the soil, and is thus available to the plant. A sequestrene called Sequestrene Plus contains manganese as well as iron. This should be applied at the rate of 1 oz. in 25 gallons of water to each 100 square feet of soil. Two or three applications are necessary between May and September. Any plant showing definite chlorosis should be given one level teaspoonful of the Sequestrene Plus which must be well watered-in. Other deficiencies in the soil and the effect they have on the leaves are shown in the accompanying illustration.

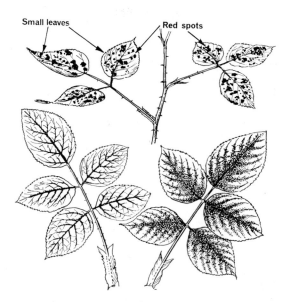

Rose leaves affected by nitrogen deficiency (top), *iron deficiency* (bottom left) *and manganese deficiency* (bottom right)

Leaf showing magnesium deficiency

Fungus or Spore diseases

Mildew. This disease attacks the foliage in early June and again in late August and early September on the young foliage. It is the commonest fungal disease of the rose and is unsightly even when the attacks are slight, and can be quite destructive if it is left unchecked and the attack becomes severe. The leaves become attacked by whitish spots which soon spread over the whole surface as a white powdery fungus. Hot days followed by cold nights when the dew formed provides sufficient water for spore germination are ideal conditions for the formation and spread of Rose Mildew. If the trees are dry at the roots the disease spreads even more rapidly. Karathane is effective if applied weekly for a few weeks after the first sign of Mildew has been noted. Care must be taken to use the prescribed strength; if a too strong solution is used, leaf scorching is almost certain to occur. Green sulphur puffed on to the leaves is also effective, as is the household washing soda sprayed at the strength of a handful in 2 gallons of soft water, though this does sometimes disfigure the leaves.

Mildewed rose tree

Black Spot. Certain districts, notably the south and south-west of England and south Wales, are more liable to attacks of Black Spot than the industrial midlands and the north. It seems to be becoming more widespread and certain varieties are more susceptible than others. The sprays we have at present are preventive and must be applied immediately after pruning and repeated at fortnightly (certainly no longer than three-weekly)

intervals during the growing season. The black spots with fringed edges do not usually appear until late June or early July, but once the attack starts it spreads rapidly. Unless rigorously controlled, the disease can completely defoliate the trees during August. Although the trees recover and make further growth during September, the cumulative effect will weaken the trees and necessitate the replacement of them. Spray the trees and beds after autumn pruning with Bordeaux mixture. This *must* be done *before* the leaves begin to form. Orthocide (Captan) or Maneb should later be applied to the foliage every three weeks (more frequently if washed off by rain). A warm, wet or humid climate where the atmosphere is free from industrial fumes is conducive to the rapid spread of the disease. It has been established that certain soil deficiencies tend to make the trees more susceptible to Black Spot. These are mainly due to shortages of the elements magnesium, boron, iron and phosphorus. The first three can be supplied by watering

Leaves showing Black Spot

the soil near the trees with a solution of 8 oz. magnesium sulphate (commercial Epsom salts), 1 oz. ferrous sulphate, ½ oz. household borax dissolved in 3 gallons of soft water applied over an area of 8 square yards. A deficiency of phosphorus can be made good by sprinkling 2 oz. super-phosphate over 1 square yard and watering in if the weather is dry. I have noted in my garden in the south-west that certain varieties, notably Allgold, Super Star, Pink Favourite, Picture and to a lesser extent Peace, are practically immune from attacks of Black Spot, although surrounded by varieties which have been completely defoliated by the disease. What a boon it would be if the plant chemists could extract the substance which makes the leaves of certain varieties immune and provide us with a systemic fungicide, such as we have in Abol X for greenfly, which could be applied to the more susceptible varieties.

Rust. This disease is especially dangerous and will kill the trees if not controlled. It appears as orange-coloured spores on the underside of the leaves in July. These spores become black in August or early September. The leaves fail to perform their function of food-building and the new shoots droop and finally shrivel. The stems carrying the buds bend over and the bud withers before it can open. Once the disease has become established the only thing to do is to dig up and burn any badly affected trees and remove and burn the leaves which are less severely attacked. Spraying with Maneb★ is an effective preventive but it must be applied *before* the attack takes place. If you have seen it on any trees in one season and these trees were not so badly affected as to have been destroyed, spray these varieties in June the following year and examine the undersides regularly to see if any orange spots appear. If they do appear, spray again with Maneb and see that the undersides of the leaves are thoroughly soaked with the fungicide. Fortunately this dis-ease is not widespread and only occurs when climatic conditions are favourable. A dry summer following a cold dry spring is conducive to the development of Rust spores.

★ Maneb 80% wettable compound is supplied by Bugge Insecticides Ltd, Sittingbourne, Kent.

7. Roses for Rock Gardens, Children's Gardens and Edging of Beds

These miniatures bear charming tiny roses of perfect shape, resembling the roses on Dresden china ornaments. Generally speaking they grow on bushes 10 ins.–12 ins. high but one very charm-ing one which must not be omitted is Cécile Brunner, which grows 2 ft.–3 ft. high and there is even a climbing variety of it bearing exquisite tiny blooms. Although not suited for edging beds, Cécile Brunner in bush form will make a charming background to the rock garden. Also, in front of Cécile Brunner, a few of the beautiful Garnette roses which reach a height of 2 ft. may be grown. These roses are similar to floribundas in that they flower in clusters.

The Garnette roses should be grown in beds enriched with farmyard manure, or failing this with a good rose fertiliser mixed with a generous amount of peat. Dig a hole large enough to take the roots without doubling them up or cramping them. Tread firmly after planting. These roses love full sun so bear that in mind when choosing the site for planting. Plant in the period Novem-ber to March when weather and soil conditions permit. Prune in March or April, but little pruning is necessary. Just cut them back to 12 ins.–18 ins. or just trim off the previous year's flowering wood to a suitable eye. The Garnette roses are quite hardy and may be regarded as medium growing floribundas. The flowers last an exceptionally long time in water and are excellent for indoor decora-tion. Good varieties are: Pink Garnette (rose pink), Rose Garnette (rose cerise), Golden Garnette (fragrant, deep yellow), Salmon Garnette (a rich deep salmon), Peach Garnette (a really charming new variety of soft peach colour) and Garnette Tiara (a new white variety).

Some *miniatures* are shown in colour facing page 57. Not only are they suitable for rock gardens and children's gardens, but form excellent subjects for window-boxes and may be grown in 7-in. pots and old sink troughs. So, however restricted the space, it is possible to grow these charming little roses.

One of the earliest miniatures was **Pompon de Paris** raised in 1839. It has very small double bright pink flowers and was formerly sold as a pot plant in the Paris markets. It is alleged that *R. roulettii* was discovered growing in pots on window ledges of Swiss cottages, whence it was introduced into commerce very early in the nineteenth century. This very pretty dwarf miniature (8 ins.–12 ins.) has double rose red flowers which are continuous over a long period.

Two other attractive varieties which match *R. roulettii* in height are Midget and Sweet Fairy. **Midget** (1941) carmine red semi-double with slight fragrance. Its fern-like leaves give it an added charm. **Sweet Fairy** (1946) apple blossom pink, semi-double and sweetly fragrant. It might strike you as curious that there is over a century gap between the production of *R. roulettii* and Pompon de Paris and that of Midget and Sweet Fairy. The reason for this is that a more economic method of production had to be found to replace the technique used formerly, of taking cuttings, rooting under glass and selling as pot plants. It was a Dutchman, de Vink, who was to show the way by using his country's long-established method of growing root-stocks under glass which allows grafting to be carried out in February, thus speeding up the 'budding' of the trees and yet keeping the dwarf habit of the miniature. The graft is a piece of the stem with one dormant bud and the attached leaf growth. This is tapered and inserted into a stock which has had all the top growth removed down to the crown. After planting out the stock and graft in peat still under glass and leaving until the callus forms between graft and stock, it is removed to a cold frame for hardening off and then planted outside. These trees are then ready to be sent out in the autumn, thus saving a year and bringing the production more in line with that of the hybrid tea roses.

In addition to the dwarf bushes there are short standards of these miniatures which can be used with effect in beds of the dwarf bushes. Other varieties varying in height from 10 to 12 ins. well worth growing are:

Baby Gold Star (1940) semi-double golden yellow which is intensified at the centre of the bloom; **Perla de Montserrat** (1945) clusters of deep pink flowers, edged with pearl; very compact, giving profuse bloom. **Pour Toi**, sometimes called **Para Ti**, and, in England, **Wendy** (1946) a lovely variety, pale ivory with a touch of yellow at the base of the petals. It is semi-double.

Presumida (**Peter Pan**) (1948) the colour varies somewhat in different soils and climate and is sometimes pale yellow (pumpkin yellow) and sometimes white with a yellowish centre. The flowers are double and are very prolific.

Rosina (**Josephine Wheatcroft**) (1951) semi-double sunflower yellow blooms in small clusters. A variety well worth growing.

Cinderella (1953) a satiny white rose tinged with pale pink. It has a spicy fragrance and blooms continuously from early June until November. A very hardy variety. **Tinker Bell** (1954) bright rose pink blooms which are small and double and cupped in shape. It only grows about 8 ins. high but is very floriferous. **Coralin** (1955) blooms a deep rose red colour, compact grower, blooms very prolifically. **Simple Simon** (1955) a deep carmine pink. The flowers are double and the growth very dwarf (6 ins.). **Baby Masquerade** (1956) a true replica of the floribunda Masquerade with abundance of tiny lemon chrome blooms which turn rose red as they develop and have a fruity fragrance. A delightful variety growing about 15 ins. high. **Dwarf king** (1957) double blooms of a deep carmine red colour which are flat when fully open. **Dian** (**Diane**) (1957), small double blooms of a deep soft red colour which have an apple fragrance.

Eleanor (1960) double flowers, coral pink deepening with age. A very free bloomer of bushy habit. **Easter Morning** (1960) sometimes called **Easter Morn** is a very beautiful white double bloom of vigorous though dwarf growth. A very choice recent introduction. **Little Flirt** (1961) a real charmer, fragrant orange red with reverse yellow blooms in great abundance. **Scarlet Gem**

(1961) a bright orange scarlet, just the variety for edging a bed of Orange Sensation, Orangeade or Sarabande. The blooms are cupped and open to a rosette formation. **New Penny** (1962) a semi-double orange red in bud opening to coral pink, a fascinating new introduction. **Yellow Doll** (1962) buds are long pointed and high centred, the flowers are double, yellow, fading to cream, and fragrant. A useful addition to the yellows.

8. Roses for Hedges

What could be nicer for that front garden hedge than suitable varieties of roses? Not only will they give beauty as well as protection to your garden, but will gladden the hearts of the passers-by. There are many suitable varieties but it is essential to prepare the soil well before planting. This is especially important if you are replacing an existing hedge of the gross-feeding privet type. In fact it will pay you in such a case to dig out the soil 18 ins. deep and replace it with some good loam. Manure well, because this hedge will be there for some time. If farmyard manure is not possible to obtain, use compost or peat and incorporate hoof and horn meal before planting. Prune hard the first year and later remove dead, unripened and thin wood. The rugosa shrubs are improved by clipping with hedge shears in the spring.

Shrubs

Sweet Briar, *R. eglanteria* or *R. rubiginosa*, is often recommended but it has a short flowering season. It is the foliage which is fragrant and for this virtue alone it is worth planting as a background to some more floriferous variety. The **Penzance Briars** are related in many cases to the Sweet Briar but most of them are subject to Black Spot where this disease is prevalent. **Meg Merrilies** is one of the best of this group. It is very fragrant and has profuse rosy single blooms in the summer. Probably the best varieties for hedges up to 5 ft. are the Pemberton 'Hybrid Musks'. Three of the best of these are **Penelope**, shell pink fading to white with a creamy yellow centre and very fragrant, foliage dark green; **Cornelia**, a strawberry pink flushed with yellow and fragrant, the foliage is dark bronze green and is leathery and glossy; **Felicia**, also fragrant, pink shaded yellow. All the three produce good recurrent bloom in the autumn and make hedges which need no supports. A more recent hybrid musk which makes an excellent hedge is **Will Scarlet**, a sport of Wilhelm or Skyrocket. The fragrant scarlet blooms are borne in trusses as are the Pemberton hybrids and it gives good recurrent blooms throughout the summer and autumn.

Hedge of Penelope

For those with larger gardens who may want a taller hedge, possibly as a screen between two parts of the garden, e.g. flower garden and vegetable garden, the rugosa hybrids are particularly good. They again are recurrent bloomers and have rich fragrance. The best varieties are **Sarah van Fleet** with its very fragrant, large semi-double pink blooms; the thick hairy leaves characteristic of the rugosa family give an added attraction. **Roseraie de l'Hay** a most charming rugosa hybrid with the characteristic foliage and crimson red, changing to rosy magenta blooms, which are richly fragrant. The double white **Blanc double de Coubert** does not give quite so much bloom in the autumn but the large white flowers during the summer, with their rich fragrance make it an attractive subject for hedges.

For those who want a really thorny hedge **Hunter** will fill the bill. It has stout stems covered throughout their length with bright crimson double blooms of medium size. It has very little fragrance, but is very free flowering. And finally, there is that attractive rugosa hybrid **F. J. Grootendorst** with slightly fragrant crimson flowers, the petals of which are fringed at the edges.

Floribundas and Ramblers

Some of the stronger growing floribundas make fine hedges. **Queen Elizabeth**, provided some of the stems are pruned to get some blooms at a lower level and the orange scarlet variety **Scarlet Queen Elizabeth**, which does not grow quite so tall; both make good hedges and produce many blooms in the autumn. **Gustav Frahm** is another vigorous type, with scarlet crimson blooms and doesn't mildew so badly as does **Frensham** in certain places. If posts and wire can be provided, the ramblers **Albertine**, **Paul's Scarlet**, **Aloha**, can be secured to the wires and make impenetrable fences.

The planting distances for the hedges should be roughly, for shrubs: 3 ft. to 4 ft.; for floribundas: 18 ins., in double rows planted in echelon; and the ramblers can be planted 4 ft. apart. Varieties are planted somewhat closer for hedges than they are in borders or beds, to ensure solidarity.

9. Roses for Indoor Decoration

In selecting roses suitable for indoor decoration, several factors are worth considering.

(*a*) If vivid coloured wallpapers are used, care must be taken to see that the colour of the roses does not clash too violently with their surroundings.

(*b*) For corner pedestals or tallish stands, large roses like Peace, even when fully open, and floribundas of the type of Scarlet Queen Elizabeth, can

be quite striking. For the sideboard or side tables, vases or bowls can be used effectively for both hybrid tea and floribunda roses, the blooms being arranged for frontal effect. The centre of a dining-table is best served by a shallow bowl with roses not so tall and large as to cut off all visibility with one's *vis-à-vis*. I have seen rose blooms floated in a shallow bowl and they give a charming effect on a small table. If, of course, one side only of the table is being occupied by diners, a larger arrangement can be used effectively on the opposite side. The length of stem used will depend upon the arrangement decided upon. Also, for shallow bowls, some of the blooms, cut with quite short stems from shrubs, e.g. Roseraie de l'Hay (purplish crimson), Blanc double de Coubert (white), Fritz Nobis (apple blossom pink), Maiden's Blush (white), amongst others, may be used with charming effect.

(*c*) The lasting power of the rose is also an important consideration, particularly to the busy housewife. It can be greatly increased by cutting the roses in the early opening stage, just as the outer petals are separating from the bud, when there will be the added joy of seeing them open. This is particularly noticeable in roses like the floribunda Lilac Charm, which when cut in the bud, opens to reveal the rich lilac colour of the petals and the golden anthers borne on red filaments, much of which is lost if the flowers are allowed to open fully out of doors. The Garnette roses (see page 27) last particularly well in water. Also certain hybrid teas, e.g. Super Star, Josephine Bruce, Gay Crusader, have long lasting powers even when cut with blooms about three-quarters open, i.e. the second and third row of petals reflexing.

(*d*) Fragrance is always an added attraction, for what can be more entrancingly stimulating than to enter a room the atmosphere of which is permeated by the sweet fragrance of roses?

HYBRID TEA ROSES
FOR INDOOR DECORATION

Angel Wings (Lindquist 1958) bright yellow base, shading to white with pink edges to the petals. Blooms are high centred and very fragrant.

Baccara (Meilland 1956) a brilliant deep vermilion, usually with a black streak on the outer petals. It is best grown under glass when the blooms are produced on long stems, and are not marred by wet. It has no fragrance, but its striking colour and exceptionally long lasting powers make it a great favourite. **Blue Moon** (Tantau 1964) has long pointed buds which open to well-formed lilac blooms which are richly fragrant and borne on long stems. This is the nearest to a true blue rose yet produced. I never thought I should like a blue rose but I adore this one, which is still pale violet rather than blue. **Eve Allen** (E. M. Allen 1964) is a charming bicolour. The blooms, which are fragrant, are a rich crimson with saffron yellow at the base of the petals and deep saffron yellow reverse. It has glossy foliage. **Grand'mère Jenny** (Meilland 1950) is light yellow with the edges of the petals flushed with pink. It is slightly fragrant and the foliage is deep green. **Grandpa Dickson** (Dickson 1965) has deep lemon yellow fragrant blooms, beautifully formed and borne on long stiff stems. The foliage is a rich green and glossy. **Lady Sylvia** (Stevens 1927) is an old favourite for indoor decoration. It has well formed delicate pink blooms, which are tinged with yellow at the base and are very fragrant. **Mojave** (Swim 1954) is a deep orange and red flame colour, of moderate size. The foliage is glossy. It has no fragrance. **Monique** (Paolino 1949) a well-shaped silvery pink rose with a touch of salmon. It is very fragrant and as it opens very quickly should be cut when the bud is just releasing its outer petals. **Montezuma** (Swim 1956) has large deep salmon-red well-formed blooms and is particularly good in the autumn. It does not like a wet summer. **Peace** (Meilland 1942) is almost too well-known to require description. The colour varies according to the locality from light yellow to deep yellow with a shading of cerise on the edges of the petals. It is magnificent when fully open and requires a suitable setting to do full justice to its beauty. **Piccadilly** (McGredy 1959) is a gay bicolour, scarlet with buttercup yellow reverse, and a slight fragrance. It has glossy dark green foliage which is reddish bronze when young.

Picture (McGredy 1932) is an old favourite and it still keeps its earlier promise. A soft pink medium sized bloom which opens to resemble a pink gardenia, but it has no fragrance. **Spek's Yellow** (Verschuren 1947) is a rich daffodil yellow and the blooms are well formed and of medium size. It often gives large trusses of good blooms which can be used effectively. **Super Star** (Tantau 1960) is an outstanding variety which lasts a long time in water. Its brilliant pure light vermilion colour is most striking, but it must be used by itself to get the best effect. It is also fragrant and the foliage which is mid-green, is disease-resistant. **Sutter's Gold** (Swim 1950) in the bud is light orange shaded and streaked with red, but when fully open the effect is distinctly yellow. It is very fragrant. The foliage is deep green and leathery. **Virgo** (Mallerin 1947) is the best garden variety for indoor decoration. Of the whites it is least affected by rain. It lasts well in water. Fragrance is very slight.

Westminster (Robinson 1959) is one of the most fragrant of the bicolours. It is cherry red, paler on the reverse, which is splashed with yellow. In addition to the hybrid teas, certain of the floribundas are useful where space permits. **Queen Elizabeth** (pink), **Scarlet Queen Elizabeth** (orange scarlet), **Allgold** (golden yellow), **Red Favourite** (velvety crimson), **Orange Sensation** (orange flame) can all be arranged with striking effect and they last quite well even if cut when fully open.

10. Roses for the Beginner

Anyone starting a collection of roses for the first time would like those which are robust, vigorous with good foliage, a good return of blooms per bush, with rapid succession of blooms. Also, he would like roses which are not too badly affected by wet and those with stiff stout stems which carry roses with their heads held proudly erect. Added to these requirements he would like his roses to be gay and bright in colour and finally, those which are fragrant.

While it is not possible to meet all these requirements in every variety named, the following selections of hybrid teas and floribundas should not disappoint the veriest tyro, but he must always remember that good cultivation is necessary if good results are to be expected. Also he must be prepared to do a certain amount of spraying to combat any of the pests or diseases which attack roses in common with other plants.

HYBRID TEAS

White

Frau Karl Druschki (Lambert 1901). This old rose is the whitest of the whites, although the outer petals do have a streak of pink. It stands up to wet better than any other white, but has no fragrance. **Pascali** (Lens 1963) is a good new white, well shaped and of moderate size. Its growth is vigorous and upright. Again it has little or no fragrance.

Pink

Lady Sylvia (Stevens 1927) is very fragrant. The blooms are a delicate pink with a touch of yellow at the base. The stems are long and stiff and well clothed with attractive foliage.

Monique (Paolino 1949) a seedling of Lady Sylvia with a richer pink colour is also very fragrant. The growth is very vigorous and upright. **Gavotte** (Sanday 1963) is a warm pink with a lighter reverse. The blooms are large and of excellent shape. The growth is vigorous and the foliage large and plentiful.

Pink Favourite (Von Abrams 1956) gives deep rose pink, large and well shaped blooms which are only slightly fragrant. The foliage is a very glossy rich green. The growth is vigorous and upright.

Helen Traubel (Swim 1951) has light warm pink touched with apricot, blooms which are very fragrant and of good form and substance. The foliage is large and of a rich green colour. **Pink Peace** (Meilland 1959) is a very vigorous grower with deep pink, large and loosely formed blooms. It has slight fragrance.

Lilac Rose (Sanday 1962) has most attractive foliage especially in the young stage and the growth is vigorous, the blooms are an unusual pink which has lilac shadings and are of good shape and substance. They stand up well to wet weather. **Stella** (Tantau 1959) is a peach pink flushed with cream and with an edging of carmine, a most attractive flower of good shape and full petalled. It does not mind rain. A splendid garden variety.

Bicolours

For sheer gaiety these are excellent value. The following are among the best and easiest to grow.

My Choice (Le Grice 1958) an attractive shade of pink with yellow at the base of the petals and a pale yellow reverse. Richly fragrant and well formed. The growth is vigorous and the foliage good and plentiful. **Eve Allen** (E. M. Allen 1964) has blooms of a rich crimson with a touch of yellow at the base of the petals and saffron-yellow reverse. It is fragrant; the growth is vigorous and the foliage glossy. **Piccadilly** (McGredy 1959) is a gay bicolour with attractive glossy, dark green foliage which is particularly attractive in the young stage when it is reddish bronze. The blooms are a rich scarlet with yellow reverse.

Rose Gaujard (Gaujard 1958) has somewhat cupped blooms which start with a high pointed centre. They are cherry red splashed with silvery white, the reverse being silvery white suffused with pale pink. The growth is very vigorous and the foliage glossy and leathery. **Miss Ireland** (McGredy 1960) a dainty bicolour of golden orange salmon with yellow reverse. It grows well and has good foliage. Only slight fragrance but a charming decorative rose.

Vermilion

Super Star (Tantau 1960) is one of the most trouble-free roses I grow. It is tall and has excellent foliage. The blooms are of perfect shape, fragrant and of a striking light vermilion colour.

Carmine and Deep Salmon

Montezuma (Swim 1956) is a deep salmon red which is at its best in the autumn. It does not like wet weather but in a dry autumn it gives of its best. A very vigorous grower with large attractive foliage. **Wendy Cussons** (Gregory 1959) is a cerise with a touch of scarlet-rose and has a very rich fragrance. The blooms are large and well formed and the growth is vigorous. **Violinista Costa** (Camprubi Nadal 1937) has orange carmine with gold shading blooms in great abundance. It is fragrant. The growth is vigorous and the stems viciously thorny.

Deep Red

Mme Louis Laperrière (Laperrière 1952) is a seedling of Crimson Glory with much of its parent's rich fragrance. It is deep crimson and of moderate size. A good garden variety with good foliage. **Ena Harkness** (Norman 1946) is a rich crimson beautifully formed bloom. Very fragrant and a fine garden variety when soil suits it. It does not do too well on heavy land. The tendency to 'nod' owing to weak flower stalk can be corrected somewhat by generous feeding. Does best in a wet season. **Uncle Walter** (McGredy 1963) under good soil conditions will reach shrub proportions, so vigorous is its growth. The colour is scarlet with crimson shading but it has little or no fragrance. Gives a generous supply of blooms and the foliage is most attractive.

Yellow

Spek's Yellow (Verschuren 1947) is a tall grower with somewhat sparse foliage. It often, particularly in the autumn, carries its rich daffodil yellow blooms in large trusses, each individual bloom being on a long stem. The colour does not fade during sunny weather. It has slight fragrance. **Sutter's Gold** (Swim 1950) has a most attractive long pointed bud which opens to a moderately large bloom. In the bud stage the outer petals are streaked with red, but when the bloom is fully open, yellow is the predominant colour. It is extremely fragrant. The foliage is deep green and leathery. The growth is upright with long flower stems. For those beginners who like to introduce at least one very new rose, they cannot do better than buy **Grandpa Dickson** (Dickson 1966). It is

a very vigorous grower with rich glossy leathery foliage and stiff flower stems. The blooms are a deep lemon yellow colour and of excellent shape. Every rose seems to be perfect in form. It is also fragrant. I think this is a rose with a great future.

FLORIBUNDAS

White

Iceberg (W. Kordes 1958) is pure white when fully open, the buds are slightly tinged with pink. It has fragrance and produces large heads of well-spaced blooms. The growth is vigorous. It is the best white floribunda so far and is continuously in flower from June to October or November.

Yellow

Allgold (Le Grice 1956) is still the best of the yellows. The blooms are a rich golden yellow and the colour is maintained until petal fall. Fragrant. The foliage is a deep green, glossy and very resistant to disease. **Golden Jewel** (Tantau 1959) is as golden as its name implies and it is slightly fragrant. The individual blooms are full and they open to about 3 ins. Each cluster bears up to ten blooms. It is moderately vigorous and has dark glossy foliage. A new variety worth trying is **Miss Delightful** (Sanday 1966). It has Masquerade as one of its parents and has that variety's strong growth. The heads of yellow blooms are large and very well spaced. The foliage is good. A good garden variety.

Pink

Poulsen's Bedder (Poulsen 1948) has moderately full rose pink blooms in small trusses. It is very free flowering and the growth is vigorous and upright. The foliage is bronzy green and glossy. **Vogue** (Boerner, Jackson & Perkins 1949) is a very fragrant variety of an attractive deep pink to carmine shade. The trusses which are large, are composed of small but perfectly formed hybrid tea roses. The growth is very vigorous and the foliage glossy. **Pink Parfait** (Swim 1962) is a most attractive variety. The individual blooms which are carried in fairly large trusses are double, high centred, small hybrid teas, of a medium to light pink with pale orange at the base of the petals. It is very free flowering and slightly fragrant. The growth is vigorous and upright and the foliage somewhat glossy. **Queen Elizabeth** (Lammerts 1955) is a very tall grower and needs judicious pruning so that at least a few of the flowers are borne at a lower level. The large double pink blooms in small trusses are very attractive and they stand up to wet weather very well. The foliage is good and large and disease resistant.

Red

Red Favourite (Tantau 1951) gives velvety scarlet crimson blooms which are not spoilt by rain. Not a tall grower, about 2 ft. to 2 ft. 6 ins., but producing large heads of well-spaced blooms. **Evelyn Fison** (McGredy 1962) is a bright scarlet with heads of well-spaced blooms. The foliage is good and the growth is robust and of medium height. **Fervid** (Le Grice 1960) gives heads of well-spaced scarlet blooms, with a touch of orange, which are semi-double and have a little fragrance. It grows well and gives a tall bush which blooms very freely. **Moulin Rouge** (Meilland 1952) is bright scarlet. The blooms are produced in large trusses and are unaffected by rain. The growth is vigorous and the foliage a mid-green colour. **Frensham** (Norman 1946) is a magnificent grower, though in some places it suffers from mildew. The light green foliage enhances the brilliant deep scarlet crimson blooms which are carried in large, well-spaced heads. Still one of the best of the reds. **Ohlala** (Tantau 1957) a rather dull scarlet-crimson paling towards the centre which is enhanced by golden stamens. The growth is very vigorous and the foliage highly resistant to disease. **Sarabande** (Meilland 1957) is a bright dazzling scarlet and has large trusses of semi-double blooms displaying golden stamens. Moderately vigorous growth and bushy. It is certainly a variety to grow. **Firecracker** (Boerner, Jackson & Perkins 1955) has blooms which are scarlet suffused with carmine and are yellow at the base. They are large and semi-double, revealing golden stamens, and have a pleasing fragrance. The habit of growth is vigorous and bushy.

Orange Red

Friedrich Heyer (Tantau 1956) is a fine growing specimen which will reach shrub proportions. The large orange red semi-double blooms are borne in large trusses. The foliage is dark, leathery and glossy. An easy variety to grow. **Lübeck** (R. Kordes 1960) is another charming orange red variety which grows to shrub proportions and therefore must be given more than the normal amount of space. The trusses are large and profuse.

Orange Scarlet

Orange Sensation (de Ruiter 1960) is a strikingly bright variety which has large well-spaced trusses of double orange vermilion blooms. The growth is vigorous and the foliage plentiful and mid-green, but like others in this colour range needs protection from Black Spot in certain areas. Has distinct fragrance. **Orangeade** (McGredy 1959) is a bright orange vermilion rather than scarlet. The semi-double blooms often come singly at first and then give large trusses of brilliant blooms. The foliage is good. May have to be sprayed against Black Spot. **Scarlet Queen Elizabeth** (Dickson 1963) is a tall growing variety, not quite as tall as the pink Queen Elizabeth, with good disease-resistant foliage. The orange-scarlet globular blooms in medium-sized trusses are particularly attractive in autumn.

Salmon

Elizabeth of Glamis (McGredy 1964) is an excellent variety, robust and bushy, producing large trusses of a rich salmon colour which are very fragrant. It blooms freely and with good continuity. **Dearest** (Dickson 1960) is a rosy salmon colour and the blooms which are highly fragrant are large in small trusses. The growth is vigorous and bushy, but the blooms do not like wet weather.

Varied Colours

Masquerade (Boerner, Jackson & Perkins 1950) is a strong growing bush with plentiful foliage and carries large heads of medium-sized blooms which start bright yellow, then turn salmon pink and finally red, all colours appearing in one head of bloom at the same time, producing a bizarre effect which appeals to some. It is certainly easy to grow. **Circus** (Swim 1956) has clusters of large double, high centred blooms which are fragrant. The colour changes from yellow marked with pink to salmon and scarlet. A good garden variety with abundant bloom and good leathery foliage. **Shepherd's Delight** (Alex. Dickson & Sons 1958) is a glorious colour, with shades of orange and red. The blooms are carried in large trusses and are semi-double. Is a strong grower with a long flowering period.

THE NEW CLIMBERS
AND SEMI-CLIMBERS

The beginner may wish to try a few of the newer climbers. The following, which give good bloom both in summer and autumn, are well worth a trial.

Pink Perpetue (Gregory 1965) is a truly perpetual flowering climber. It will grow on walls, fences, pergolas or posts and produces exquisite pink blooms in great profusion. The blooms are in small clusters and are double. **Golden Showers** (Lammerts 1957) has long pointed buds which open to large double flowers produced singly or in clusters along the stem. They are daffodil yellow, and are produced in great quantity throughout the summer and autumn. **Casino** (McGredy 1963) has large, double, soft yellow blooms well formed and fragrant. It blooms freely during summer and autumn. The foliage is dark and glossy. A vigorous semi-climber. **Joseph's Coat** (Armstrong Nurseries 1964) is a yellow and red multi-coloured variety with large double blooms recurring throughout the whole season. It makes an excellent pillar rose. **Royal Gold** (Morey 1957) has few equals in rich deep yellow climbers, but may need a little protection against frost in the colder climates. The hybrid-tea-shaped blooms are produced well into the autumn. It does extremely well on a post and grows to a height of 7 ft. with good cultivation. **Leverküsen** (Kordes 1955) gives sprays of lemon yellow blooms which open to large full flowers from pointed buds. The foliage is light green and glossy. Will make an excellent pillar rose up to 8 ft. It is truly recurrent.

Autumn Sunlight (Gregory 1965) is a recurrent climber of unusual and attractive colour in a climber, orange vermilion. The blooms are globular and grow in clusters. The foliage is bright green and glossy and the growth is very free. It is also free flowering and repeats well.

11. Increasing your Stock by Cuttings and by Budding

Cuttings

Many varieties may be increased quite easily from cuttings, e.g. ramblers, climbers, shrub roses, floribundas and strong-growing hybrid teas. The chief advantage of increasing your stock by cuttings is that, the tree being on its own roots, one is never troubled with suckers. Another one is that it is a comparatively simple process. The disadvantages compared with budding on a root-stock are (*a*) it takes longer to get a strong tree which will bear a good crop of blooms, and (*b*) only one new tree per stem is obtained, whereas one stem may provide three or four or even more buds for budding and therefore subsequent new trees. This enables you to increase your stock without weakening unduly the parent tree.

The cuttings may be taken by pulling off a side shoot 4 ins.–6 ins. long with a 'heel'. Hold the shoot close to the stem with finger and thumb and pull downwards towards the base, leaving a length of the parent stem attached to the heel shoot. The best time to do this is July or August, when the wood is half ripe. The attached part of the parent stem is then pared with a sharp knife and finally the tail is cut off with secateurs, leaving about $\frac{1}{2}$ in. of the old wood. Finally, the lower leaves are removed and the leaf-buds in the axils of these leaves (i.e. the points where the leaf stalk joins the stem) are rubbed out leaving one or two leaves at the tip of the shoot. These cuttings can then be inserted in very sandy loam, watered and kept out of direct sun. They must never be allowed to dry out but must not be over-watered.

Another method which is quite effective is to select well ripened young stems, i.e. of the current season's growth, in September or October, and cut them off cleanly just below a leaf-bud near the base. The cuttings should be about 12 ins. long and about the thickness of an ordinary pencil. The cut below the leaf-bud should be horizontal and a sloping cut should be made just above the top 'eye' or leaf-bud. The lower eyes should be

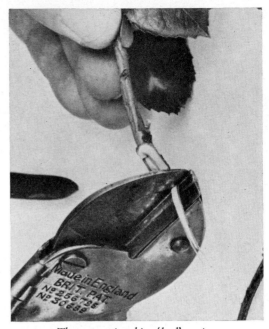

Three stages in taking 'heel' cuttings

rubbed out or removed by cutting out with a sharp knife (see illustration below).

A V-shaped trench, 8 ins.–9 ins. deep, is then

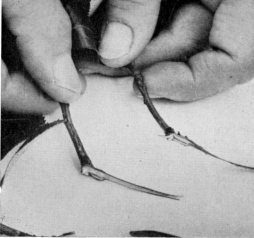

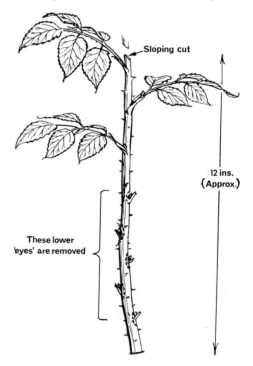

prepared and the bottom 2 ins. covered with damp sand. The cuttings, which are placed 6 ins. apart, are pushed into the sand until the bottom of the cutting is in contact with the base of the trench. The stems should rest on the slightly sloping back of the trench while the soil is replaced and finally pressed firmly on both sides with the foot, so that the cuttings are in close contact with the soil. Prior to putting the cuttings in position, the lower end may be moistened on damp cotton wool or blotting paper and then dipped into a hormone producing powder, Seradix B. The hormone helps in the formation of roots.

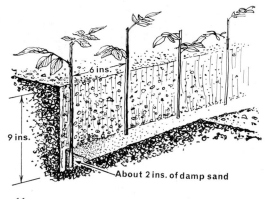

Budding

If you have the time, it is well worth while trying to bud a few rose trees on a suitable root-stock, or understock. The variety of root-stock chosen depends to a large extent on the type of soil in your garden and, to a lesser extent, on the variety of the rose budded. On rich loamy soils, somewhat on the 'heavy' side—and these are fairly common in Britain—the best understock is probably R. *canina* in the seedling form. On 'light' sandy loam it is often found that R. *multiflora* or R. *laxa* gives better results, and there are other varieties which are reputed to suit certain roses, e.g. Polmeriana—which is a thornless R. *canina*—is said to suit yellow roses. My own experience on heavy land is that R. *canina*, seedling briar, is a good all-purpose understock. The suitability of understocks is still the subject of research and is of far too great a scope to be discussed here.

Seedling briars, or other understocks, can be obtained fairly cheaply from certain nurserymen whose advertisements appear from time to time in the horticultural journals and papers. If you only need a small number your own nurseryman

A typical seedling briar. Those with straight stems or necks are easier to bud

Prepare a trench 9 ins. deep so that the roots can be laid in. Plant stocks in winter at 1-ft. spacing to give sufficient working space when budding

will probably supply you if you speak to him in the early autumn. The *process* of budding is the same for all root-stocks and the following general instructions will serve for any variety.

The seedlings should be planted as soon as they arrive in November, December, or even January,

The base of the root-stock when the soil has been removed, showing the portion where the bud is inserted in June or July. The original soil level is indicated by a line

After planting, firm the soil evenly around the stocks. If more than one row is being planted, space the rows at 2 ft. apart

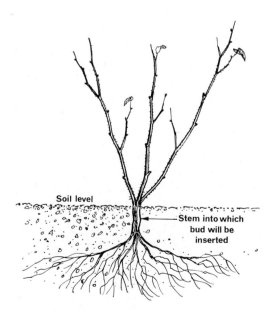

Take buds from young shoots cut from flowering bushes in June or July. The shoots should be stood in water until required. Remove leaves but not the leaf stalks

unless the ground is frostbound. They should be planted about 12 ins. apart in well-prepared beds, the short stretch of stem between the roots and the many thin branches being just covered with soil. They must then be allowed to grow naturally and if the spring is dry they will be helped considerably by an occasional soaking with water. The budding time is determined by the ripeness of the stems from which the leaf-buds are taken and the flow of sap in the understock. The former is indicated by the ease with which thorns can be flicked off the stem which has just borne a good bloom. If the thorns just bend over, the wood is not sufficiently ripe, and if they persist in adhering to the stem the wood is too old and too hard. The understock is ready if the bark comes away easily and the surface of the wood underneath is moist with flowing sap. Before you start operations, get together in a garden trug: secateurs, budding

knife, a sharpening stone so that the knife blade can be sharpened from time to time, raffia cut into lengths about 15 ins. long and moistened by

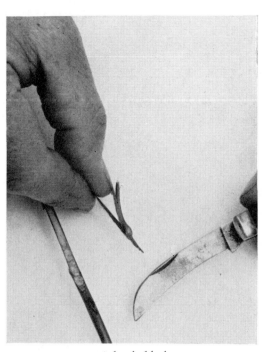

A detached bud

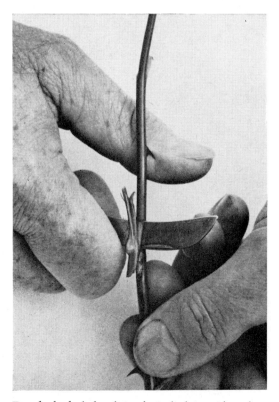

Detach the buds by slicing beneath them with a sharp knife. Use only stout, well-formed buds

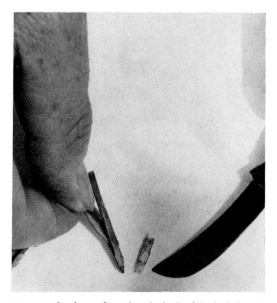

Remove the sliver of wood at the back of the bud cleanly. The intact leaf stalk forms a convenient handle

dipping into water and squeezing out the surplus water, a duster, a jam-jar containing water an inch deep in which the stems will stand until the buds are taken from them, and a garden trowel. Ease the soil away from the stems of the understocks to be budded, using the trowel and being careful not to damage the bark.

Now all is ready. Cut off the leaves from the

Make a T-cut in the stock at the lowest point possible, after removing 1–2 ins. of soil

Open up the lips of the T with the handle of the budding knife to allow for easy insertion of the bud

Form the top of the T first, then make a downward cut about 1¼ ins. in length

Insert the bud into the T-cut. Leave the leaf stalk—this will rot away after the bud has taken

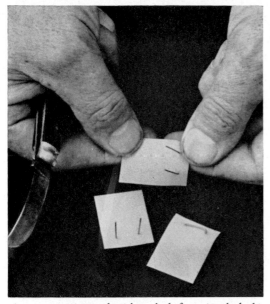

A very convenient and quick method of securing the bud is to use thin rubber patches with two thin wire spikes protruding from the staple

An alternative method is to use moist wide raffia. Bind around the bud above and below

Place the patch in position over the bud and secure by the wire spikes. The patch should be left in place to rot away

Tying completed above and below the bud. When growth from the bud starts in spring, slit the raffia to release it. Cut off the portion of the root-stock above the inserted bud in mid-February stems selected, but leave about an inch of the leaf stalk to serve as a handle. Stand the stems in the water in the jam-jar.

For preference take the buds from the middle of the stem as those near the top are often too advanced and those near the base not sufficiently developed. Remove the bud by slicing beneath it with the sharp blade of the budding knife, starting $\frac{1}{2}$ in. below the bud, slightly changing the angle of the blade when just behind the bud, and finally, with the raised bark and its attached thin sliver of wood held between the thumb and the blade of the knife, give a quick pull and a long tail of bark will come away from the stem. Now hold the tail of bark in the left hand, insert the thumbnail of the right hand under the end of the whitish sliver of wood, and gently remove the sliver from the bud. The tail is then cut off, leaving about $\frac{1}{2}$ in. above the bud. The exposed stem of the understock is cleaned by rubbing it with the duster. Make a T-cut in the bark, starting with the top of the T and then cutting downwards about 1 in. or $1\frac{1}{4}$ ins. if the stem is long enough. The bark is lifted with the flat part of the handle of the budding knife and the bud inserted. This must be done as quickly as possible as neither the bud nor the exposed part of the understock must be allowed to become dry. The beginner will find it useful to hold the bud between the lips while the T-cut is being made. Be careful to put the bud the right way up when slipping it under the raised bark of the understock. Secure the bud either by tying-in with the prepared raffia or using thin rubber patches with thin wire staples attached. The beginner may find raffia easier to manage but both methods are illustrated in the diagrams. If raffia is used the ties should be examined after a fortnight and if they appear to be too tight, thus preventing sap from rising, they should be eased. The thin rubber patches are sufficiently elastic to allow for any swelling as the bud develops, and finally, the growing bud will pierce the rubber. A thin cane should be inserted so that the young shoot or shoots can be tied to it to prevent the new growth being blown out before it is firmly attached to the wood of the understock. Do not cut away the top growth of the root-stock until mid-February, when it is cut

away cleanly with the secateurs about $\frac{1}{2}$ in. above the bud, which by this time should be swelling and showing signs of life. If the bark of the original bud is still green you may be practically certain the bud has 'taken', but if it has gone brown and shrivelled, the bud is probably dead.

When June arrives you will have a maiden tree showing signs of flowering and often the best blooms are given by these maiden trees. The trees can be transplanted from their budding quarters

in the autumn and pruned in the next spring. In early summer these 'cut-backs' will bloom quite freely.

Budding standards or half-standards is done in exactly the same way, but 4 ft. 6 ins. or 2 ft. 6 ins. above the ground respectively. The popular stock to use is R. rugosa which is budded on the main stem, and two or three buds may be inserted symmetrically round the stem. Thin canes should be tied to the upper part of the standard so that the young shoots may be tied-in to prevent them being blown out at an early stage. If standard briars (R. canina) are used, the buds are inserted as near the main stem as possible, in the laterals which have been allowed to develop at the required height, one bud in each lateral. All growths from the main stem below the buds must be removed, but the head of the stock whether R. rugosa or R. canina, is not removed until the following February. R. rugosa standards should be budded in June, R. canina in July or early August.

12. Making New Roses

Propagation by cuttings or by budding merely increases the number of trees of a given variety. To create a new rose is quite a different matter. But how fascinating!

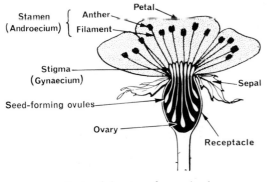

Sectional drawing of a rose head

Before attempting this method of propagation (hybridising, it is called), it will be helpful to understand the function of the various parts of a flower. The essential organs concerned with hybridisation are those which produce the sexual cells. They are the male and female parts of a flower. The male organ is named the *androecium* and consists of stamens. A stamen is composed of two parts: an anther, which contains pollen sacs filled with pollen, and a thin stalk, called a filament, which supports the anther. The female organ is named the *gynaecium* or pistil, the sticky top of which is called the stigma. From this sticky top several tubes, called styles, pass down into a receptacle and at the lower ends of the styles are situated the ovules, where the seeds are formed. The swollen part which contains the ovules is called the ovary. The non-essential organs of the flower comprise the sepals, petals and nectaries. When pollen is transferred from the anthers to the stigma the operation is called *pollination*. If the pollen from the anthers of a given rose falls on, or is transferred by other means to, the stigma of the same flower, the process is called self-pollination. If, on the other hand, the pollen from one rose is

transferred to the stigma of another variety, this is called cross-pollination. This transference of pollen may be carried out quite indiscriminately by the wind or bees, and seeds will result, but there is no assurance that any good roses will result from these seeds although occasionally a good one may emerge. The hybridists work more scientifically. They carefully select parents with characteristics they wish to develop. Even then, they cannot guarantee success and very few from a large batch of seedlings will be worth further cultivation.

For the benefit of the amateur who wishes to indulge in this fascinating game, the following is a brief description of the method to adopt. First select the roses you wish to use as (a) the male, and (b) the female parent. The rose chosen as the female should have the petals removed by using a pair of long pointed scissors, before the flower is open. This exposes the stamens and the stigma and as the latter is the organ to be used the stamens are all cut away just above the receptacle. The stigma is now left to develop for a day or two, often covered with a small polythene bag to protect it from pollen which may be blown on it from surrounding flowers. The rose chosen as the male parent has been allowed to open wide and the pollen sacs to ripen. The yellow dust which drops from the pollen sacs is ripe and ready to be applied to the sticky top of the stigma. This may be done by using a camel-hair brush or rabbit's tail or even the finger. It is important to wait until the top of the stigma is sticky before applying the pollen. Germination of the pollen grains is started by the sticky substance on the stigma, when pollen tubes grow from the pollen grains. The formation of a pollen tube may be seen by viewing, through a microscope, pollen grains placed on a drop of sugar solution on a glass slide. The conducting tissues of the style enable the pollen tube to reach the ovary and it is here that some of the tube's contents pass into the ovule. It is the ripened ovule which is the seed. This combination of male and female gametes is called fertilisation. The female gamete is generally known as the oösphere or egg cell and after fertilisation by the male cell it becomes the oöspore. The fertilised egg or seed is possessed of the characters of both parents thus increasing its

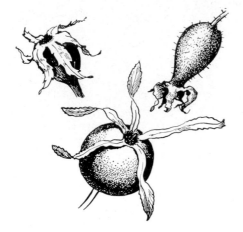

send six trees to the Royal National Rose Society's Trial Grounds at St Albans, Hertfordshire, where after two years or possibly three, it will be considered for an award.

Time and patience are required in this process of making new roses, but if it is ever rewarded by receiving a gold medal of the R.N.R.S. it will have been well worth while and, in any case, will have provided an absorbing hobby for the amateur rose-grower.

variability. The seeds are contained in the ripened receptacle—the familiar rose-hip.

The ripened rose-hips are collected, probably in October, and buried in moist peat in a seed-pan or box. This seed-pan is kept out of doors but must be protected against mice as these animals have a special liking for rose seeds. When the fleshy part of the rose-hip has rotted, the seeds can easily be extracted. The seeds should be sown about 1 in. apart and about ½ in. below the surface of the sterilised soil. John Innes seed compost is the best sterilised soil mixture for the amateur. Sow the seeds in January or February in the greenhouse kept at a temperature of about 55°F.

You will get some seedlings springing up in March or April, other seeds will take much longer to germinate, some may even take up to eighteen months—so don't be too eager to throw away the contents of the seed-pan.

When the seedlings have grown their first true leaves, transplant into another seed-box spacing them wider apart and allow them to flower. This is when you get your first thrill, but do not be too optimistic. Many of the seedlings will be quite useless, but there may be one or two which are worth potting-on in 5-in. pots in a slightly richer soil— John Innes No. 1 or No. 2 potting compost. After a second flowering, if they show sufficient promise, bud them on a suitable understock, say seedling briar, and grow them in the open garden. It is then that you can assess the merits of the rose. If you feel you have an exceptionally good rose,

13. Growing Roses in the Small Greenhouse

More and more garden-lovers are buying a small greenhouse in which they can potter during the dark evenings or when the weather is not conducive to outdoor work. It can be used to propagate seedlings of various types for bedding-out plants, also in the autumn it can be used for chrysanthemums, in the winter and early spring for roses and

A wooden greenhouse, size 12 ft. 6 ins. by 8 ft. 3 ins. Optional staging (both sides) can be obtained at extra cost

*A wooden greenhouse, size 10 ft. by 8 ft., for erection on a
brick base*

gives much more freedom as regards a suitable
height for the pots used for different purposes. A
table can always be put at one end on which to
grow the seedlings if required. It will be helpful,
though not essential, to have some form of controlled heating which will require the minimum
of attention and will switch itself on and off at the
required temperatures (or within a few degrees of

*A Minibrite 8 ft. by 8 ft. standard aluminium alloy house
erected and glazed ready for use. This one is on a wooden
base, but brick or concrete is more usual. Note that
maximum light is admitted in this type of house*

in the summer for tomatoes. The greenhouse need
never be unoccupied. The type of greenhouse
most likely to meet with favour is one in which all
the above can be grown in their season. Here we
are particularly concerned with roses, and they
can be grown well in any of the three ridge-type
houses illustrated, or they may be grown in a
lean-to of the type shown. I would advise the
purchase of a house without fixed staging, as it

A lean-to type greenhouse

*A fan heater can be fitted with a thermostat, thus ensuring
that electricity is not wasted. When the temperature
reaches the required level, the heater is shut off
automatically*

Electrical tubular heaters are available in several sizes. Here a double tier is being used, but these heaters can be used singly or trebly as required. Doubles and trebles are controlled by a thermostat

these temperatures); in other words, a thermostatically controlled heater. There is much to be said for either an electric fan heater or electric tubular heater, thermostatically controlled. If electricity is installed, an electric light point will be useful for work during the dark evenings.

If the greenhouse is to be used for growing other crops in the summer and autumn it is advisable to grow the rose trees in pots for ease of removal. If the greenhouse has a wooden or brick

Lining the inside of a greenhouse with heavy-gauge polythene sheeting can give 5–10 extra degrees of heat. Always line the ventilators separately to ensure adequate ventilation

base, arrange a low staging so that the tops of the pots just reach the bottom of the glass in the sides. If the house has glass practically to ground-level, the pots can stand on a bed of sand or cinders. It is essential to keep all windows clean so that as much light as possible can reach the trees. Also see that you have some sort of fittings that will enable you to line the inside quickly and easily with heavy-gauge polythene sheeting during cold weather, covering the ventilators separately for easy open-

For early flowering in a greenhouse most H.T. and Floribunda roses can be potted into 10-in. pots in autumn. Roots may need to be trimmed and carefully spaced in the pots

ing. It is also possible to install a device which will control the ventilators by opening or closing the windows automatically. Two such devices are called *Thermofor* and *Autovent*.

To start a collection

Pot up trees from the garden in October or November in 10-in. pots. The bottom inch of the pot is filled with broken pieces of unglazed plant pots. This is covered with 2 ins. of good loam enriched with powdered old dry manure and a tablespoonful of bonemeal. Trim the roots of the trees to fit the pot neatly and use a good potting compost, e.g. John Innes No. 3. Alternatively, some seedling briars can be potted up in the same way, left standing out of doors and budded in

July as described on pages 39–42. These latter can be brought into the greenhouse at the beginning of December after the budding, and the heads of the briars cut off at the end of the month. Trees that are potted up from the garden are best left to grow in the pots out-of-doors, pruned in March, allowed to flower in the summer just as they would have done in the garden and then brought into the greenhouse at the beginning of December. The aim is to have the pots full of roots before feeding and slightly forcing indoors. Both methods take the same length of time before the pots are brought into the greenhouse and both give good results. Half or quarter standards budded on *R. rugosa* also give good results.

Roses need fairly firm potting and a rammer can be used for this purpose. A suitable compost is 3 parts loam, 2 parts peat and 1 part coarse sand (by bulk). The pots should be taken into the greenhouse in early winter

The trees are pruned hard towards the end of December and no artificial heat should be given before mid-January. The roof ventilators should be kept open so that there will be free circulation of air and even if there is a sharp frost no harm will be done. On bright and sunny days still more ventilation may be given from the roof. In early

February the trees will break into leaf, and frost should be excluded by use of the polythene sheeting and if necessary a little artificial heat, but the ventilators must be kept open slightly. The aim should be to prevent the temperature falling below 45°F. at night or rising above 60°F. in the daytime. Careful attention must be given to watering. It must not be overdone nor must the trees be allowed

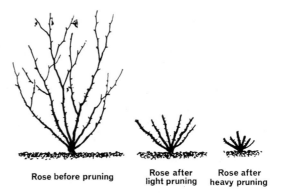

Rose before pruning   **Rose after light pruning**   **Rose after heavy pruning**

to dry out. Daily spraying with soft water helps to keep the young foliage clean and as soon as any greenfly is noticed add a little Abol Derris to the water. During February, watering the pots twice a week should be ample. Towards the end of the month weekly watering with chemical fertilisers will be necessary. I have found 'Wellgro' a simple and adequate food given once a week until the second week in March, and then twice a week when the flower-buds first appear.

During March the temperatures should be kept as near as possible to 60°F. at night and 70°F. by day. It is during April that your skill as a rose-grower will be really tested, for occasionally the temperature will run up to 100°F. at mid-day and unless you are careful with the heating, will drop below 50°F. at night. Polythene sheeting helps considerably. Careless ventilation and rapid changes in temperature usually result in an attack of Mildew. Use the precautions mentioned on pages 25–26 as soon as any sign of Mildew appears. Caterpillars can also be troublesome and must be picked off by hand. They are easily spotted by their habit of curling themselves in the young leaves near the flower-bud. Side buds should be removed if large flowers are required. Remove all except one at a very early stage, the one being left in case anything untoward happens to the main bud.

Towards the end of April and during May, your efforts will be rewarded by superb blooms of a quality rarely seen in the open garden.

After the first blooms have been cut, the trees are gradually cooled off preliminary to their removal to the open in June. During the summer and autumn the trees are left to bloom as they will, being watered occasionally. The pots will not dry out so easily if they are stood in a trench, dug in some part of the garden. It will help to keep the roots within bounds and protect from invasion of worms if pots are stood on pieces of slate. In October the pot-rose year begins again. The pots are cleaned and examined for drainage, weeds and worms and the top inch of soil replaced just before bringing them into the greenhouse, by a top dressing of the compost originally used in potting-up, enriched with a teaspoonful of bonemeal per pot.

any suckers that may have been overlooked. See that any new beds that may be required for planting are thoroughly prepared and prepare the planting soil mixture so that the trees can be planted as soon as possible after arrival. Clean out the greenhouse when the crop of tomatoes or chrysanthemums is finished, so that it will be ready to house the pot roses at the right time. If painting the inside of the greenhouse is necessary, now is the time to do it.

15. A Selection of Roses

The list of roses selected has been arranged in alphabetical order, the type (hybrid tea, H.T.; floribunda, Flor., etc.) being inserted after the variety named. The name of the raiser and the year of its introduction into commerce are also

14. Jobs for the Autumn

When the flowering season is over, a certain amount of tidying up is necessary. Rake off and burn all leaves from the beds. This is very important if the trees have suffered from spore diseases during the summer. Remove all remaining dead heads and seed pods and at the same time shorten any long stems on the hybrid teas and the flori-bundas so that rocking and twisting in the wind, with the consequent root damage, can be reduced to a minimum. Give a last clean-up of weeds. Prune ramblers and tie the new shoots to the supports. Check all stakes and ties of the standards as these are very liable to damage in the winter storms. Trim the shrub roses and cut out dead or useless stems. Remove from their point of origin

Alamein

given together with a brief description of each variety.

Alain. *Flor.* (Meilland 1948). *Blooms:* medium sized, bright carmine red, semi-double in large clusters. *Foliage:* dark and glossy. *Growth:* upright and bushy.

Alamein. *Flor.* (S. McGredy 1963). *Blooms:* semi-double, flat and deep scarlet or mauve red in clusters. *Foliage:* dark green. *Growth:* vigorous.

Albéric Barbier. *Rambler* (Barbier 1900). *Blooms:* yellow, double, in clusters, fading to creamy white in sunlight. *Foliage:* glossy and dark. *Growth:* very vigorous giving profuse bloom in summer only.

Albertine

Albéric Barbier

Albertine. *Rambler* (Barbier 1921). *Blooms:* coppery pink, opening from reddish salmon buds, fragrant and in small clusters. Very profuse summer blooming. *Foliage:* mid-green and plentiful. *Growth:* a very vigorous rambler.

Alison Wheatcroft. *Flor.* (Wheatcroft Bros. 1959). *Blooms:* apricot flushed crimson, semi-

double in open clusters. *Foliage:* dark and glossy. *Growth:* vigorous, giving plentiful bloom.

Allen Chandler. *Large-flowered Climber* (Prince 1923). *Blooms:* vivid bright crimson, large and semi-double in clusters of 3 or 4 blooms in summer only. *Foliage:* dark and glossy. *Growth:* suitable for pillar or tall weeping standard.

Allgold

Allgold. *Flor.* (Le Grice 1956). *Blooms:* large heads of rich yellow semi-double flowers which do not fade at all. *Foliage:* small, dark and glossy. *Growth:* vigorous and bushy. (See plate on previous page.)

Allgold. *Climbing Flor.* (Gandy 1961). A climbing variety similar in other respects to the bush form.

Allotria. *Flor.* (Tantau 1958). *Blooms:* large semi-double orange scarlet in compact clusters. *Foliage:* dark and glossy. *Growth:* vigorous, tall and upright.

Aloha. *Large-flowered Climber* (Boerner, Jackson & Perkins 1955). *Blooms:* large, double, deep rose pink with deeper reverse and recurring well in autumn. *Foliage:* dark and leathery. *Growth:* very vigorous, will reach 8–10 ft. on pillar.

Ambrosia

Aloha

Ambrosia. *Flor.* (Alex. Dickson & Sons 1962). *Blooms:* medium sized, dark amber, in large clusters, semi-double opening flat. *Foliage:* dark green. *Growth:* vigorous and bushy.

American Pillar. *Rambler* (Dr Van Fleet 1902). *Blooms:* large, single, carmine pink with white eye and golden stamens, in large clusters on long strong stems giving red fruits. Flowers only in summer. *Foliage:* glossy, mid-green. *Growth:* vigorous, suitable for arch or pergola.

André le Troquer. *H.T.* (Mallerin 1950).

American Pillar

Blooms: large, double, cupped, very fragrant, and orange shading to apricot. *Foliage:* dark green. *Growth:* vigorous and upright giving abundant bloom.

Angel Wings. *H.T.* (Lindquist 1958). *Blooms:* large and high centred, bright yellow at the base, shading to pale yellow or white, with pink edges, very fragrant. *Foliage:* leathery. *Growth:* vigorous and upright.

Anna Wheatcroft. *Flor.* (Tantau 1959). *Blooms:* light vermilion, single with golden stamens in large heads of well spaced blooms; very free flowering. Has slight fragrance, but the great attraction is the colour. *Foliage:* dark and glossy. *Growth:* vigorous and bushy.

Anne Watkins

Anne Letts. *H.T.* (Letts 1953). *Blooms:* large and well formed, of specimen bloom standard and a delicate pale pink with an even paler reflex. Needs protection against rain. *Foliage:* deep green and glossy. *Growth:* very vigorous and with very thorny stems.

Anne Watkins. *H.T.* (Watkins Roses 1962). *Blooms:* well shaped, large, apricot shaded yellow with deep apricot reverse. *Foliage:* dark and glossy. *Growth:* vigorous and upright.

Apricot Nectar. *Flor.* (Jackson & Perkins 1965). *Blooms:* perfectly shaped hybrid-tea type of a light apricot colour. *Foliage:* light green and glossy. *Growth:* vigorous and bushy.

Apricot Nectar

Apricot Silk. *H.T.* (Gregory 1965). *Blooms:* high centred, large double, and of a rich apricot colour. *Foliage:* dark and glossy. *Growth:* vigorous and tall.

Apricot Silk

Arthur Bell. *Flor.* (S. McGredy 1965). *Blooms:* large semi-double and very fragrant, are yellow to creamy yellow. Clusters are well spaced. *Foliage:* attractive heavily veined. *Growth:* vigorous and bushy and carrying much bloom. (Col. pl. facing p. 56.)

August Seebauer. *Flor.* (Kordes 1950). *Blooms:* of hybrid-tea type growing in clusters; deep rose pink. *Foliage:* dark and glossy. *Growth:* very vigorous giving profuse bloom.

Autumn Sunlight. *Large-flowered Climber* (Gregory 1965). *Blooms:* double, medium sized and orange vermilion in clusters. *Foliage:* bright green and glossy. *Growth:* very free, makes a good pillar rose. (Col. pl. between pp. 56 and 57.)

Aztec. *H.T.* (Swim 1957). *Blooms:* large from long pointed buds, double, high centred and scarlet orange in colour. *Foliage:* deep olive green and leathery. *Growth:* vigorous and spreading.

Baccara. *H.T.* (Meilland 1956). *Blooms:* deep vermilion with dark streak on outer petals, medium size, no fragrance, lasts a long time as a cut bloom. It is excellent under glass. *Foliage:* dark and leathery. *Growth:* not too good out-of-doors, upright and bushy under glass.

Bettina

Bacchus. *H.T.* (Alex. Dickson 1951). *Blooms:* double, well formed, moderate sized, cherry red and fragrant. *Foliage:* rich dark green. *Growth:* very vigorous and upright. Does best with light pruning.

Baden-Baden. *H.T.* (Kordes 1952). *Blooms:* double, moderate sizes, rich deep scarlet crimson, very fragrant and well formed. *Foliage:* dark and leathery but somewhat sparse. *Growth:* vigorous and upright.

Beauté. *H.T.* (Mallerin 1954). *Blooms:* large double, long pointed and shapely, of an orange yellow colour with touches of deep apricot. *Foliage:* deep green and plentiful. *Growth:* vigorous and bushy.

Bettina. *H.T.* (Meilland 1953). *Blooms:* large, double, well formed salmon orange, veined with red. *Foliage:* glossy bronze green but in some areas liable to Black Spot. *Growth:* vigorous.

Betty Uprichard. *H.T.* (Alex. Dickson 1921). *Blooms:* large, semi-double, fragrant, delicate salmon pink with carmine reverse. *Foliage:* light

Beauté

green, glossy and leathery. *Growth:* very vigorous and tall, giving profuse bloom.

Blanc double de Coubert. *Hybrid Rugosa* (Cochet-Cochet 1892). *Blooms:* large, semi-double, flat, extremely fragrant and white.

Blanc double de Coubert

Bloomfield Abundance

Foliage: thick hairy shining dark green and very decorative. *Growth:* very vigorous, and of shrub proportions.

Blaze. *Large-flowered Climber* (Kallay 1932). *Blooms:* semi-double in small clusters, bright scarlet. *Foliage:* dark and leathery. *Growth:* very vigorous, makes a good pillar rose.

Bloomfield Abundance. *Chinensis Shrub* (Thomas 1920). *Blooms:* very small, double, salmon pink, similar to Cécile Brunner but slightly larger. *Foliage:* dark and glossy. *Growth:* vigorous and bushy. Will make a good specimen shrub.

Blue Diamond. *Flor.* (Lens 1964). *Blooms:* hybrid-tea type in small clusters, lavender mauve in colour. *Foliage:* dark and coppery. *Growth:* vigorous, compact and bushy.

Blue Diamond

Blue Moon. *H.T.* (Tantau 1964). *Blooms:* lilac, double, with high pointed centre and very fragrant. *Foliage:* good and plentiful. *Growth:* very vigorous with long flower stems. (See plate overleaf.)

Bond Street. *H.T.* (S. McGredy 1965). *Blooms:* large and well shaped, pink with deeper pink at edges, quite fragrant and will need quite a lot of disbudding for large blooms but can be grown as a small truss of blooms. *Foliage:* mid-green. *Growth:* vigorous and upright.

Bonn. *Shrub* (Kordes 1949). *Blooms:* semi-double, orange scarlet, with musk fragrance. *Foliage:* light green. *Growth:* very vigorous, makes a good specimen shrub (6 ft.).

Bonny Maid. *Flor.* (Le Grice 1952). *Blooms:* semi-double, large, deep pink with paler reverse, in small trusses. *Foliage:* large, dark and leathery. *Growth:* vigorous and bushy.

Buccaneer

Blue Moon

Border Coral. *Flor.* (De Ruiter 1958). *Blooms:* semi-double, coral salmon in large well spaced trusses, free flowering and fragrant. *Foliage:* dark and glossy. *Growth:* vigorous and spreading.

Brilliant. *H.T.* (Kordes 1952). *Blooms:* very large, well formed, rich scarlet, little fragrance. *Foliage:* dark green. *Growth:* fairly vigorous, but very subject to Mildew. An exhibitor's rose. (Col. pl. between pp. 56 and 57.)

Buccaneer. *H.T.* (Swim 1953). *Blooms:* rich buttercup yellow, medium sized and moderately full. *Foliage:* dark green and leathery. *Growth:* very vigorous, will reach shrub proportions, too tall for bedding but makes a good shrub.

Carla. *H.T.* (De Ruiter 1963). *Blooms:* large, double, apricot yellow, suffused evenly with pink, a lovely soft colour. *Foliage:* dark and glossy.

Growth: vigorous, particularly good under glass where blooms do not suffer through rain.

Casino. *Climbing H.T.* (McGredy 1963). *Blooms:* yellow in bud, somewhat paler on

Casino

Celebration

There is also a climbing variety which is similar in all other respects.

Celebration. *Flor.* (Alex. Dickson 1961). *Blooms:* salmon pink, in small trusses of large full and well shaped blooms which are reasonably fragrant. *Foliage:* light green. *Growth:* vigorous and bushy.

Champs Elysées. *H.T.* (Meilland 1957). *Blooms:* full and well formed, rich velvety crimson, do not mind rain. *Foliage:* good and plentiful. *Growth:* vigorous and bushy.

Chanelle

opening to full and shapely flowers. *Foliage:* dark and glossy. *Growth:* vigorous, is a good semi-climber 7–8 ft. and gives good recurrent bloom.

Cécile Brunner. *Hybrid China Floribunda* (Ducher 1880). *Blooms:* Exquisitely formed miniature blooms of a pale shell pink opening to almost white rosette shaped flowers in well spaced trusses. *Foliage:* rather sparse, soft and dark green. *Growth:* vigorous, will make a good shrub if pruned lightly.

Champs Elysées

Chanelle. *Flor.* (McGredy 1958). *Blooms:* large, semi-double of hybrid-tea type in large well spaced clusters, peach pink with an underlay of cream. *Foliage:* dark and glossy. *Growth:* vigorous and bushy.

Chaplin's Pink Companion. *Climber* (Chaplin 1961). *Blooms:* fairly full, fragrant, silvery pink rosette form in clusters up to 30. *Foliage:* glossy, mid-green. *Growth:* vigorous, producing blooms in summer only. (See plate overleaf.)

Charles Gregory. *H.T.* (Verschuren 1948).

Chaplin's Pink Companion

Charleston

Blooms: vermilion shaded gold, very fragrant, medium sized, of good shape. *Foliage:* dark and glossy. *Growth:* vigorous, a good bedding variety.

Charles Mallerin. H.T. (Meilland 1947). *Blooms:* deep velvety crimson, large, but opening rather flat, very fragrant. *Foliage:* leathery and dark green. *Growth:* only moderate, needs good cultivation.

Charleston. *Flor.* (Meilland 1963). *Blooms:* large, semi-double, yellow flushed with crimson and finally becoming crimson, fair-sized cluster. *Foliage:* dark, leathery, glossy. *Growth:* dwarf and bushy.

Charlotte Elizabeth. *Flor.* (Norman 1965). *Blooms:* deep pink with red edges, high centred, of hybrid-tea type in good clusters. *Foliage:* glossy. *Growth:* vigorous and branching producing a good bush.

Charlotte Elizabeth

Charlotte Wheatcroft. *Flor.* (Wheatcroft Bros. 1957). *Blooms:* single, borne in well spaced large trusses and bright scarlet in colour. *Foliage:* dark and glossy. *Growth:* vigorous, tall.

Charm of Paris. *Flor.* (Tantau 1965). *Blooms:* of hybrid-tea type, large and well formed, salmon pink in moderate clusters. *Foliage:* abundant, dark green. *Growth:* vigorous, giving a bush 3 ft. high. (See plate page 57.)

Chicago Peace. H.T. (Johnston 1962). *Blooms:* phlox pink with yellow base, large rather cup-

▲ GRANDPA DICKSON, H.T.

▲ OHLALA, FLOR.

▲ EVE ALLEN, H.T.

▲ SUPER STAR, H.T.

▲ FRIEDRICH HEYER, FLOR.

▲ EVELYN FISON, FLOR.

◀ ORANGE SENSATION, FLOR.

ARTHUR BELL, FLOR. ▶.

▲ SUTTER'S GOLD, H.T.

ROSE DE MEAUX, *R. centifolia pomponia*
▼

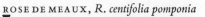

▲ MAIGOLD, SHRUB OR CLIMBER

▲ SILVER LINING, H.T.

▲ BRILLIANT, H.T.

▲ LEVERKÜSEN, KORDESII CLIMBER

◄ MISS DELIGHTFUL, FLOR.

MEG, LARGE-FLOWERED CLIMBER ▶

▲ ELIZABETH OF GLAMIS,
FLOR. STANDARD

▲ PINK PARFAIT, FLOR.

▲WENDY CUSSONS; H.T. STANDARD

▲ AUTUMN SUNLIGHT,
LARGE-FLOWERED CLIMBER

▲ STELLA, H.T.

▲ LUCY CRAMPHORN, H.T.

▲ GAVOTTE, H.T.

◄ DEAREST, FLOR.

PINK PERPETUE,►
LARGE-FLOWERED CLIMBER

▲ SCARLET GEM, MINIATURE

▲ EASTER MORN, MINIATURE

▲ ELEANOR, MINIATURE

▲ TINKER BELL, MINIATURE

▲ YELLOW DOLL, MINIATURE

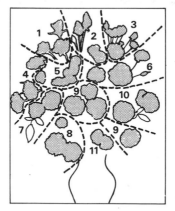

▲ LITTLE FLIRT, MINIATURE

Key to composite, opposite below left

1. ROSINA
2. POUR TOI
3. GRANATE
4. DWARF KING
5. PRESUMIDA
6. CORALIN
7. DIANE
8. BABY MASQUERADE
9. CINDERELLA
10. BABY GOLD STAR
11. PERLA DE MONTSERRAT

NEW PENNY, MINIATURE ▶

Charm of Paris

Chinatown

shaped, double, with little fragrance. *Foliage:* leathery and glossy. *Growth:* vigorous, upright and bushy.

Chinatown. *Shrub* (Poulsen 1963). *Blooms:* rich yellow with touch of pink as bloom ages, well formed and produced in small clusters. *Foliage:* mid-green, glossy. *Growth:* very vigorous and tall.

Chicago Peace

Christian Dior

Christian Dior. *H.T.* (Meilland 1959). *Blooms:* large, double, high centred and crimson flushed scarlet. *Foliage:* leathery and glossy. *Growth:* very vigorous, upright and tall. (See plate on previous page.)

Christopher Stone. *H.T.* (Robinson 1934). *Blooms:* large, full, dark velvety scarlet overlaid crimson, very fragrant. *Foliage:* bright green. *Growth:* moderately vigorous.

Chrysler's Imperial. *H.T.* (Lammerts 1952). *Blooms:* large, well formed vivid deep crimson apt to blue when cut; very full petalled and very fragrant. *Foliage:* large, dark green. *Growth:* moderately vigorous and compact. Needs protection against Mildew.

City of Leeds. *Flor.* (McGredy 1965). *Blooms:* semi-double, large, in well spaced trusses and rich salmon colour. *Foliage:* large dark green. *Growth:* vigorous, upright and bushy.

Colour Wonder

City of Leeds

Cocktail. *Shrub* (Meilland 1957). *Blooms:* single, geranium red with base of petals primrose yellow, spicy fragrance, always in bloom (except in winter). *Foliage:* leathery and glossy. *Growth:* vigorous, makes good shrub or may be trained as a semi-climber.

Colour Wonder. *H.T.* (Kordes 1965). *Blooms:* Nasturtium red sheathed with buttercup yellow.

Crimson Conquest

Very full petalled. *Foliage:* plentiful and healthy. *Growth:* Strong and sturdy and of medium height.

Copenhagen. *Climbing H.T.* (Poulsen 1964). *Blooms:* very full, well pointed and scarlet, are recurrent. *Foliage:* coppery. *Growth:* vigorous, makes an excellent semi-climber.

Copper Delight. *Flor.* (Le Grice 1956). *Blooms:* well spaced trusses of deep orange yellow semi-double flowers with slight fragrance. *Foliage:* olive green. *Growth:* vigorous, upright, bushy.

Cornelia. 'Hybrid Musk' *Shrub* (Pemberton 1925). *Blooms:* in large trusses of strawberry pink, semi-double, very fragrant flowers. *Foliage:* dark bronze, leathery. *Growth:* very vigorous, giving abundant and recurring bloom.

Crimson Conquest. *Climber* (Chaplin 1931). *Blooms:* in trusses of deep scarlet, single or semi-double flowers. *Foliage:* light green. *Growth:* vigorous, suitable for pillar, arch or pergola. Summer flowering only.

Crimson Glory. *H.T.* (Kordes 1935). *Blooms:* deep velvety crimson of good shape and substance, but fading badly with age, very fragrant and free flowering if pruned lightly. *Foliage:* leathery. *Growth:* very vigorous, bushy and spreading. There is also a climbing variety (Miller 1941), which produces an abundance of large, perfectly shaped blooms.

Crimson Shower. *Rambler* (Norman 1951). *Blooms:* semi-double, small, crimson, lasting well into September. *Foliage:* light green and glossy. *Growth:* vigorous, good as weeping standard.

Daily Sketch. *Flor.* (McGredy 1960). *Blooms:* of hybrid-tea type, double, in small clusters, pink and silver. *Foliage:* dark green. *Growth:* vigorous and bushy.

Dainty Maid. *Flor.* (Le Grice 1938). *Blooms:* silvery pink with carmine reverse, semi-double, large trusses of well spaced flowers. *Foliage:* deep green and large. *Growth:* vigorous, tall and bushy.

Danse du Feu. *Large-flowered Climber* (Mallerin 1954). *Blooms:* orange scarlet, opening flat, very free flowering and recurrent. *Foliage:* bronzy and glossy. *Growth:* vigorous climber 8–10 ft. suitable for pillar or walls.

Dearest. *Flor.* (Alex. Dickson 1960). *Blooms:* large, rosy salmon, opening flat, very fragrant, in

Daily Sketch

small trusses; does not like rain. *Foliage:* dark and glossy. *Growth:* vigorous and bushy. (Col. pl. between pp. 56 and 57.)

De Meaux. *R. centifolia pomponia* (Sweet 1789). *Blooms:* light rose, fragrant, small, full. *Foliage:* mid-green. *Growth:* erect. (Col. pl. between pp. 56 and 57.)

Diamant. *Flor.* (Kordes 1962). *Blooms:* full and shapely, bright orange scarlet in small trusses. *Foliage:* dark and glossy. *Growth:* vigorous and upright.

Diamant

Dickson's Flame. *Flor.* (Alex. Dickson 1958). *Blooms:* semi-double opening large in moderate-sized trusses, pure scarlet. *Foliage:* good and plentiful. *Growth:* vigorous and bushy.

Dickson's Flame

Dr A. J. Verhage. *H.T.* (Verbeek 1960). *Blooms:* apricot yellow, moderately large and of good shape with high pointed centre. *Foliage:* deep green. *Growth:* out-of-doors moderate but much better under glass. Needs good cultivation.

Dr W. Van Fleet. *Rambler* (Van Fleet 1910). *Blooms:* pale pink, medium-sized hybrid-tea form, fragrant, summer flowering only. *Foliage:* rich green and glossy. *Growth:* vigorous, suitable for pergola or screen.

Doreen. *H.T.* (Robinson 1950). *Blooms:* rich orange yellow, moderately full, large and plentiful. *Foliage:* bronzy green, very liable to Black Spot and needs protection. *Growth:* fairly vigorous.

Dorothy Peach. *H.T.* (Robinson 1956). *Blooms:* yellow flushed with pink, large, full petalled and of good shape, fragrant. *Foliage:* dark and glossy but rather small. *Growth:* vigorous and tall.

Dorothy Wheatcroft. *Flor. Shrub* (Tantau 1960). *Blooms:* large trusses of bright oriental red with darker shadings. *Foliage:* bright green and large. *Growth:* very vigorous making a good specimen shrub.

Dortmund. *Kordesii Climber* (Kordes 1955). *Blooms:* red with white eyes, large and single in large clusters, recurrent. *Foliage:* dark green and glossy. *Growth:* moderately vigorous, making a good pillar rose to 8 ft.

Dortmund

Dusky Maiden. *Flor.* (Le Grice 1947). *Blooms:* semi-double in small clusters, deep velvety crimson scarlet with golden anthers. *Foliage:* dark green but rather sparse. *Growth:* moderately vigorous.

Easlea's Golden Rambler. *Rambler* (Easlea 1932). *Blooms:* rich yellow with touches of

Dorothy Peach

Dusky Maiden

Elmshorn

crimson in clusters on long stems. Summer flowering only. *Foliage:* abundant olive green. *Growth:* rampant, suitable for pergola or screen.

Eden Rose. *H.T.* (Meilland 1950). *Blooms:* large, well formed, rich deep pink and very fragrant. *Foliage:* bright glossy dark green. *Growth:* very vigorous, ranking in quality with that of its parent Peace. This should be borne in mind when planting or it may overshadow its neighbours.

Elmshorn. *Shrub* (Kordes 1950). *Blooms:* large clusters of small double light crimson flowers. *Foliage:* wrinkled, light green. *Growth:* vigorous, tall and branching.

Eden Rose

Elizabeth of Glamis. *Flor.* (McGredy 1964). *Blooms:* a most attractive and unusual colour, salmon with peach shading, large well spaced trusses of double flat flowers with good fragrance. *Foliage:* mid-green. *Growth:* vigorous and bushy but compact. (Col. pl. between pp. 56 and 57.)

Ena Harkness

Emily Gray. *Rambler* (Williams 1916). *Blooms:* in clusters of deep golden buff flowers on long strong stems. *Foliage:* very glossy dark green, almost evergreen. *Growth:* very vigorous, suitable for pergola, arch or wall. Must be lightly pruned otherwise there will be little bloom.

Ena Harkness. *H.T.* (Norman 1946). *Blooms:* bright crimson scarlet, of good form and substance, apt to bend the head unless richly cultivated, fragrant. *Foliage:* good. *Growth:* vigorous and upright. A climbing sport (Murrell 1954), is moderately vigorous and produces large well-formed blooms. (See plate on previous page.)

Ernest H. Morse. *H.T.* (Kordes 1965). *Blooms:* large, of good form and substance, rich turkey red, very fragrant. *Foliage:* dark green and plentiful. *Growth:* very robust, 3 ft. 6 ins. A fine new variety which will please the exhibitor.

Ernest H. Morse

Ethel Sanday. *H.T.* (Mee 1952). *Blooms:* of excellent form and substance, a light yellow flushed with apricot. *Foliage:* dark green. *Growth:* vigorous and bushy.

Etoile de Hollande. *H.T.* (Verschuren 1919). *Blooms:* deep red, full and very fragrant. *Foliage:* rather sparse. *Growth:* moderate, should be lightly pruned to give height. The climbing variety

(Leenders 1931) is very vigorous and very free flowering. It gives some repeat blooms.

Etude. *Large-flowered Climber* (Gregory 1965). *Blooms:* deep rose pink, in clusters of medium-sized semi-double flowers. *Foliage:* light green and glossy. *Growth:* good, suitable for pillar 8–10 ft. Recurrent bloom.

Europeana

Europeana. *Flor.* (De Ruiter 1963). *Blooms:* large, double, rosette shaped, dark crimson in large clusters. *Foliage:* bronze green. *Growth:* vigorous and bushy.

Eve Allen. *H.T.* (E. M. Allen 1964). *Blooms:* large, double, fragrant rich crimson with saffron yellow at base and on reverse. *Foliage:* glossy, dark green, bronze reverse. *Growth:* vigorous, very free bloom. (Col. pl. facing p. 56.)

Evelyn Fison. *Flor.* (McGredy 1962). *Blooms:* vivid red with scarlet shading, large well spaced trusses. *Foliage:* rich dark green. *Growth:* vigorous and bushy. (Col. pl. facing p. 56.)

Excelsa. *Rambler* (Walsh 1909). *Blooms:* double, large clusters of bright rosy crimson flowers, summer flowering only. *Foliage:* rich glossy green.

Fandango

Growth: vigorous, suitable for pergola or arch and makes an excellent weeping standard.

Fairlight. *Flor.* (Robinson 1965). *Blooms:* large, semi-double (22 petals), long lasting, moderately fragrant, flowers in good trusses, in the bud the colour is coppery orange opening to rich deep pink with salmon shadings. *Foliage:* coppery green, dark green at the base. *Growth:* vigorous and upright.

Fandango. *H.T.* (Swim 1949). *Blooms:* Turkey red with yellow base, buds of good shape opening to semi-double flowers some $4\frac{1}{2}$ ins. across.

Fashion

Foliage: large, dark green and leathery. *Growth:* vigorous, upright and bushy.

Fashion. *Flor.* (Boerner, Jackson & Perkins 1947). *Blooms:* a rich orange salmon, in large clusters, well spaced. *Foliage:* subject to rust in some areas and must be sprayed. *Growth:* moderately vigorous and bushy.

Faust. *Flor.* (Kordes 1956). *Blooms:* hybrid-tea type, large, golden yellow with pink shading in large trusses. *Foliage:* deep green. *Growth:* vigorous, upright, tall.

Firecracker

Felicia. 'Hybrid Musk' (Pemberton 1928). *Blooms:* large trusses, salmon pink with yellow shading and recurrent bloom, the flowers are double and very fragrant. *Foliage:* good. *Growth:* vigorous, will make a bush 6 ft. tall.

Fervid. *Flor.* (Le Grice 1960). *Blooms:* semi-double, scarlet with touch of orange in large trusses. *Foliage:* glossy and dark. *Growth:* vigorous and upright. Very free bloom.

Firecracker. *Flor.* (Boerner, Jackson & Perkins 1955). *Blooms:* large, semi-double, fragrant, light scarlet with yellow base in small trusses. *Foliage:* large, light green. *Growth:* vigorous and bushy.

First Choice. *Flor. Shrub* (Henry Morse 1958). *Blooms:* fiery orange scarlet with yellow centre, single, in moderate-sized trusses, fragrant. *Foliage:* good and plentiful. *Growth:* vigorous, reaching shrub proportions; makes a good specimen bush.

F. J. Grootendorst. *Rugosa Shrub* (De Goey 1918). *Blooms:* in clusters of small double crimson flowers with fringed edges. *Foliage:* wrinkled, rather small, leathery. *Growth:* vigorous, will reach a height of 6 ft. but can be pruned to height required.

Flamenco. *Flor.* (McGredy 1960). *Blooms:* large double (21 petals) opening flat in small clusters and of a salmon red colour, very free flowering. *Foliage:* good, dark green. *Growth:* vigorous and bushy.

Fragrant Cloud

François Juranville. *Rambler* (Barbier 1906). *Blooms:* bright salmon pink in small clusters, good fragrance. Gives some repeat blooms in autumn. *Foliage:* small and bright green. *Growth:* vigorous, suitable for pergola, arch or weeping standard.

Frau Karl Druschki. *H.T. type* (P. Lambert 1901). *Blooms:* very large, double, dead white when open, tinged with carmine pink in bud, no fragrance. *Foliage:* mid-green. *Growth:* very vigorous and strong, makes a large bush.

Flamenco

Forward. *H.T.* (Le Grice 1962). *Blooms:* big and of good shape, warm primrose yellow. *Foliage:* good. *Growth:* upright and prolific flowering variety.

Fragrant Cloud. *H.T.* (Tantau 1964). *Blooms:* coral red becoming geranium red, of good form and substance, very fragrant, particularly good in autumn. *Foliage:* dark and glossy. *Growth:* very vigorous and upright.

François Juranville

Frau Karl Druschki

Frensham. *Flor.* (Norman 1946). *Blooms:* deep scarlet crimson, semi-double in large well spaced trusses. *Foliage:* bright green and abundant, subject to Mildew. *Growth:* very vigorous and spreading. Makes a fine hedge if sprayed against Mildew.

Frensham

Friedrich Heyer. *Flor. Shrub* (Tantau 1956). *Blooms:* large, semi-double, orange red, in well spaced large trusses. *Foliage:* dark green, glossy and leathery. *Growth:* vigorous and upright. (Col. pl. facing p. 56.)

Fritz Nobis. *Hyb. spinosissima shrub* (Kordes 1940). *Blooms:* pale pink with reddish salmon reverse, very fragrant, small clusters, summer flowering in profusion. *Foliage:* mid-green, glossy. *Growth:* vigorous, tall, long branching stems.

Fritz Thiedemann. *H.T.* (Tantau 1960). *Blooms:* brick red, large, full-petalled, slightly fragrant. *Foliage:* dark green. *Growth:* moderately vigorous and bushy.

Fritz Thiedemann

Frühlingsgold. *Hyb. spinosissima shrub* (Kordes 1937). *Blooms:* large, semi-double light yellow and fragrant, plentiful in summer, a few only later. *Foliage:* large, light green and wrinkled. *Growth:* vigorous, makes a large shrub. (See plate overleaf.)

Frühlingsmorgen. *Hyb. spinosissima shrub* (Kordes 1941). *Blooms:* cherry pink with soft yellow centre, single, stamens maroon, free flowering in May and June, but often early blooms are damaged in bud stage by cold winds. *Foliage:* dark green. *Growth:* vigorous long arching stems, 6 ft. (See plate overleaf.)

Gail Borden. *H.T.* (Kordes 1956). *Blooms:* high centred, deep rose pink with reverse overcast with cream. *Foliage:* deep green. *Growth:* very vigorous and upright. (See plate overleaf.)

Frühlingsgold

Gail Borden

Garvey. *H.T.* (McGredy 1960). *Blooms:* soft peach pink to rosy salmon, double, globular, fragrant, carried on strong stems. *Foliage:* mid-green. *Growth:* vigorous and upright.

Gavotte. *H.T.* (Sanday 1963). *Blooms:* warm pink with silvery reverse, large, full petalled and of good shape, fragrant. *Foliage:* rich green, large and plentiful. *Growth:* vigorous and tall. (Col. pl. between pp. 56 and 57.)

Frühlingsmorgen

Garvey

Gay Crusader. *H.T.* (Robinson 1948). *Blooms:* orange scarlet with deep yellow reverse, large and of good shape, lasts well when cut, fragrant. *Foliage:* bronzy green and glossy. *Growth:* moderate.

Gay Crusader

Gertrude Gregory. *H.T.* (Gregory 1957). *Blooms:* large, double, high centred, bright golden yellow, fragrant. *Foliage:* deep green. *Growth:* strong and bushy.

Gold Crown. *H.T.* (Kordes 1960). *Blooms:*

Gold Crown

very deep yellow, full and shapely. *Foliage:* deep green. *Growth:* very vigorous and upright.

Golden Dawn. *H.T.* (Grant 1929). *Blooms:* very large, pale buff yellow apt to split, very fragrant. *Foliage:* very good and plentiful. *Growth:* strong and bushy. Prune lightly. Several climbing sports of this variety have been produced, the latest by Le Grice 1947. This is moderately vigorous (8 ft.) and produces a wealth of bloom in summer.

Cl. Golden Dawn

Golden Giant. *H.T.* (Kordes 1960). *Blooms:* golden yellow, very full but needs much disbudding to get first class flowers. *Foliage:* light green. *Growth:* very vigorous, very tall, not suitable for bedding. (See plate overleaf.)

Golden Jewel. *Flor.* (Tantau 1959). *Blooms:* large, fragrant, double, golden yellow, in clusters (up to 10 flowers). *Foliage:* dark green. *Growth:* moderately vigorous and bushy. (See plate overleaf.)

Golden Giant

Golden Melody

Golden Jewel

buds, semi-double, opening flat. Very free flowering and good recurring bloom. *Foliage:* dark
green and glossy. *Growth:* moderately vigorous,
makes a good pillar rose, 8 ft.

Golden Showers

Golden Melody. *H.T.* (La Florida 1934).
Blooms: pale buff yellow, certainly not golden,
of very good shape and substance and rich fragrance. *Foliage:* rather sparse. *Growth:* vigorous
and spreading.

Golden Showers. *Large-flowered Climber* (Lammerts 1957). *Blooms:* golden yellow, long pointed

Golden Slippers. *Flor.* (Von Abrams 1961). *Blooms:* rich deep orange with gold reverse in medium-sized trusses, moderately full, opening into large semi-double flowers. *Foliage:* leathery and glossy, mid-green. *Growth:* compact bush.

Golden Slippers

Goldgleam. *Flor.* (Le Grice 1966). *Blooms:* large with good pointed buds, cream flushed rosy pink at the edges of petals. *Foliage:* dark green and plentiful. *Growth:* vigorous.

Goldgleam

Goldilocks. *Flor.* (Boerner, Jackson & Perkins 1945). *Blooms:* deep yellow fading to cream, in clusters, full and fragrant. *Foliage:* glossy. *Growth:* moderately vigorous and making a compact

dwarf bush. There is a climbing variety by the same raiser 1954, a sport of the floribunda, with large clusters and recurrent flowering.

Grace de Monaco. *H.T.* (Meilland 1956). *Blooms:* very large, double, well formed, globular, and very fragrant, light rose pink colour. *Foliage:* good and plentiful. *Growth:* vigorous and branching.

Grace de Monaco

Grand'mère Jenny. *H.T.* (Meilland 1950). *Blooms:* large, double, high centred, light yellow edged with pink. *Foliage:* deep green. *Growth:* vigorous but not so vigorous as its parent Peace.

Grand'mère Jenny

Grandpa Dickson. *H.T.* (Alex Dickson & Sons 1966). *Blooms:* full petalled and of excellent shape, mostly one per stem but increasing number of side buds later in the season, lemon yellow fading to cream with age, edges of petals have touches of pink particularly in the older blooms. Slightly fragrant. *Foliage:* dark green, leathery. *Growth:* vigorous and upright. (Col. pl. facing p. 56.)

Grootendorst Supreme. *Hyb. rugosa shrub* (F. J. Grootendorst 1936). *Blooms:* a deeper crimson red than F. J. Grootendorst, of which it is a sport, otherwise similar (see F. J. Grootendorst).

Guinée. *Climbing H.T.* (Mallerin 1938). *Blooms:* large, well formed, double, very fragrant, very dark scarlet with black shading, on long stems, free recurring. *Foliage:* mid-green and leathery. *Growth:* vigorous, suitable for pillar or walls, even if facing north or north-east.

Gustav Frahm. *Shrub* (Kordes 1958). *Blooms:* semi-double, scarlet crimson, in large tight trusses. *Foliage:* light green. *Growth:* very vigorous and upright.

Hamburg. *Shrub* (Kordes 1935). *Blooms:* semi-double in clusters, deep crimson, good recurrent flowering. *Foliage:* large, leathery, glossy. *Growth:* vigorous, an erect specimen bush of 6 ft.

Hamburger Phoenix. *Kordesii Climber* (Kordes 1955). *Blooms:* large, semi-double, crimson, in clusters. *Foliage:* deep green and glossy. *Growth:* vigorous, will make a good pillar rose to 9 ft. or a bushy shrub. A recurrent bloomer.

Hansestadt Bremen. *Flor.* (Kordes 1960). *Blooms:* very large, very full, in large trusses, deep salmon pink. *Foliage:* leathery. *Growth:* very vigorous, upright and bushy.

Happy Anniversary. *Flor.* (Delbard 1962). *Blooms:* moderately full salmon pink, in medium-sized trusses, fragrant. *Foliage:* deep green and glossy. *Growth:* vigorous and upright.

Happy Event. *Flor.* (Alex Dickson & Sons 1964). *Blooms:* large semi-double, cherry red with yellow reverse and at the base of the petals. *Foliage:* dark green, large and plentiful. *Growth:* vigorous and upright—almost a shrub.

Hector Deane. *H.T.* (McGredy 1938). *Blooms:* double, high centred, very fragrant, brilliant salmon carmine with yellow at the base of the

Happy Event

petals. *Foliage:* dark and glossy. *Growth:* very vigorous but compact and bushy.

Heidelberg. *Large-flowered Climber or Shrub* (Kordes 1958). *Blooms:* large, double, high centred, bright crimson with lighter reverse, in clusters. *Foliage:* glossy and leathery. *Growth:* vigorous, makes a good pillar rose or tall shrub.

Helen Traubel. *H.T.* (Swim 1951). *Blooms:* full and of good shape, bud high pointed, finally opening flat, pink to apricot, very fragrant. *Foliage:* large and plentiful. *Growth:* very vigorous and tall.

Helen Traubel

Highlight

Highlight. *Flor.* (Robinson 1956). *Blooms:* full, in large trusses, orange scarlet, free flowering, especially good in autumn. *Foliage:* dark green, large and plentiful. *Growth:* very vigorous and upright.

High Noon. *Semi-climber* (Lammerts 1946). *Blooms:* deep lemon yellow, semi-double, loosely

High Noon

cupped, fragrant and recurrent. *Foliage:* leathery, glossy. *Growth:* moderately vigorous, makes a good pillar rose 6 ft.

Honeymoon. *Flor.* (Kordes 1959). *Blooms:* rosette shaped, double medium sized, canary yellow clusters, small, up to 5 blooms. *Foliage:* dark green and veined. *Growth:* vigorous.

Hugh Dickson. *H.T. type* (Hugh Dickson 1904). *Blooms:* full, rather globular but can be high centred, very fragrant, deep scarlet crimson. *Foliage:* mid-green, rather sparse. *Growth:* very vigorous; can be trained on walls as a climber, pruning lightly and occasionally cutting down old wood to the base.

Ice White

Iceberg. *Flor.* (Kordes 1958). *Blooms:* slightly tinged with pink in the bud, but quite white when open, good shape, double in large trusses, fragrant. *Foliage:* small, light green. *Growth:* very vigorous, bushy and branching.

Ice White. *Flor.* (S. McGredy 1966). *Blooms:* of hybrid-tea form in bud, opening to double, rather flat blooms, white with edges tinged with pink in the bud stage, rather similar to Iceberg. *Foliage:* dark green and plentiful. *Growth:* vigorous and upright.

Ideal Home. *H.T.* (Laperrière 1960). *Blooms:* full and shapely, fragrant carmine pink with base white. *Foliage:* fairly good, deep green. *Growth:* vigorous and upright. (See plate overleaf.)

Innisfree. *Flor.* (Alex. Dickson & Sons 1965). *Blooms:* tangerine orange in the bud, gradually deepening from mid-carmine to deep rose as the flower matures. Medium-sized trusses. *Foliage:* pale lime green. *Growth:* vigorous, well balanced and bushy.

Irene of Denmark

Ideal Home

pink with silvery reverse. *Foliage:* dark, glossy and ample. *Growth:* tall and upright.

Isobel Harkness. *H.T.* (Norman 1957). *Blooms:* double, fragrant, bright yellow, well formed, strong stems. *Foliage:* dark and leathery. *Growth:* moderate. Liable to Black Spot.

Innisfree

Ivory Fashion

Irene of Denmark. *Flor.* (Poulsen 1951). *Blooms:* full, medium sized, white, slightly fragrant in large, well spaced trusses. *Foliage:* rather small and sparse. *Growth:* vigorous and bushy.

Isabel de Ortiz. *H.T.* (Kordes 1962). *Blooms:* well formed, high centred, full, fragrant, deep

Josephine Bruce

Josephine Bruce. *H.T.* (Bees 1952). *Blooms:* long pointed, good shape and substance, deep velvety crimson scarlet, very fragrant. *Foliage:* deep green, subject to Mildew. *Growth:* bushy and rather sprawling.

Joseph's Coat. *Semi-climber* (Armstrong 1964). *Blooms:* moderately full, golden yellow flushed cherry red at the edges of petals, shaded and veined orange. *Foliage:* mid-green. *Growth:* tall, with branching habit. Makes a good shrub or a medium pillar rose (6 ft.).

June Park. *H.T.* (Bertram Park 1958). *Blooms:* full and shapely, particularly good in autumn when it often gives a number of first class blooms on one stem, richly fragrant, pink. *Foliage:* mid-green and adequate. *Growth:* strong but rather sprawling.

Ivory Fashion. *Flor.* (Boerner, Jackson & Perkins 1957). *Blooms:* ivory white, large in medium-sized clusters, fragrant, good in autumn. *Foliage:* leathery, medium green. *Growth:* moderately vigorous.

John Church. *Flor.* (McGredy 1964). *Blooms:* large, double, well formed, orange scarlet, fragrant, in good trusses. *Foliage:* medium green. *Growth:* vigorous and tall but rather irregular.

Karl Herbst

Karl Herbst. *H.T.* (Kordes 1950). *Blooms:* large, well formed, very full petalled, deep red, at their best in a dry sunny season. *Foliage:* mid-green and leathery. *Growth:* vigorous and tall.

King's Ransom. *H.T.* (Morey 1961). *Blooms:* large, double, high centred, rich yellow, fragrant. *Foliage:* mid-green, glossy and leathery. *Growth:* moderately vigorous and tall.

Köln am Rhein. *Kordesii Climber* (Kordes 1957). *Blooms:* deep pink, large but not a good

Joseph's Coat

shape, recurrent bloom. *Foliage:* dark and glossy. *Growth:* vigorous pillar up to 8 ft. or makes a large bush.

Köln am Rhein

Konrad Adenauer. *H.T.* (Tantau 1954). *Blooms:* velvety crimson and of good shape and substance, very fragrant. *Foliage:* light green and liable to Mildew. *Growth:* vigorous and upright.

Konrad Adenauer

Korona. *Flor.* (Kordes 1953). *Blooms:* bright orange scarlet in large tight trusses, semi-double. *Foliage:* rather sparse. *Growth:* vigorous and tall.

Lady Belper. *H.T.* (Verschuren 1948). *Blooms:* light orange yellow with buff shading, full and shapely, fragrant. *Foliage:* dark and glossy but rather sparse. *Growth:* moderately vigorous.

Lady Seton. *H.T.* (McGredy 1965). *Blooms:* medium sized, clear rose-pink, well shaped in bud and fragrant. *Foliage:* medium sized mid-green. *Growth:* vigorous and bushy.

Korona

Lady Sonia. *Shrub* (Mattock 1960). *Blooms:* deep golden yellow, semi-double, large (4 ins. when wide open). *Foliage:* dark green. *Growth:* vigorous, upright and branching.

Lady Sylvia. *H.T.* (Stevens 1927). *Blooms:* full, shapely, long pointed light pink with yellow at the base of the petals, very fragrant. *Foliage:* mid-green and plentiful. *Growth:* very vigorous. Excellent under glass.

Lady Zia. *H.T.* (Bertram Park 1959). *Blooms:* very full but often split, light orange red, best in the autumn. *Foliage:* dark green and glossy. *Growth:* vigorous.

La Jolla. *H.T.* (Swim 1954). *Blooms:* large, double, high centred, fragrant. *Foliage:* deep green and glossy. *Growth:* moderate and upright.

Lady Zia

Lancastrian. *H.T.* (Gregory 1965). *Blooms:* large double, very fragrant, crimson scarlet on strong stems. *Foliage:* light green. *Growth:* vigorous and upright.

Leverküsen. *Kordesii Climber* (Kordes 1955). *Blooms:* semi-double, attractively shaped, pale yellow, recurrent. *Foliage:* light green, glossy. *Growth:* vigorous, suitable for pillar or wall. (Col. pl. between pp. 56 and 57.)

Lilac Charm. *Flor.* (Le Grice 1961). *Blooms:* large trusses of single or semi-double lilac flowers with golden anthers on scarlet filaments, fragrant. *Foliage:* large, mid-green. *Growth:* short, bushy.

Lilac Rose

Lilac Rose. *H.T.* (Sanday 1962). *Blooms:* large, full, good shape, pink with lilac shading, fragrant. *Foliage:* most attractive bronze-green when young, deep green later. *Growth:* strong and bushy.

Lilac Charm

Lilli Marlene

Lilli Marlene. *Flor.* (Kordes 1959). *Blooms:* scarlet crimson, large, semi-double in moderately sized trusses. *Foliage:* leathery. *Growth:* vigorous and well branched. (See plate on previous page.)

Lively. *H.T.* (Le Grice 1959). *Blooms:* pale carmine, well formed, exhibition type, fragrant. *Foliage:* dark green. *Growth:* compact, short.

Lively

Lübeck. *Flor. Shrub* (Reimer Kordes 1960). *Blooms:* orange red, large, double, in large trusses, well spaced. *Foliage:* dark green. *Growth:* very vigorous and tall. Good for hedges.

Lucy Cramphorn. *H.T.* (Kriloff 1960). *Blooms:* signal red, well formed, large, fragrant. *Foliage:* glossy. *Growth:* vigorous and upright. (Col. pl. between pp. 56 and 57.)

Mme Butterfly. *H.T.* (Hill 1918). *Blooms:* good form and substance, very fragrant, pale pink tinted gold. *Foliage:* rather sparse. *Growth:* vigorous and bushy. The climbing sport of this variety (Smith 1926) is free flowering in summer with some bloom in the autumn, very vigorous.

Mme Caroline Testout. *H.T.* (Pernet-Ducher 1890). *Blooms:* full and globular, warm pink. *Foliage:* rich green and soft. *Growth:*

Mme Butterfly

Mme Henri Guillot

vigorous and bushy. The climbing sport of this variety (Chauvry 1902) is very vigorous and gives a good repeat flowering in autumn.

Mme Henri Guillot. *H.T.* (Mallerin 1938). *Blooms:* deep orange scarlet suffused with salmon pink, large, moderately full, pleasing shape.

Mme Kriloff

Foliage: mid-green, large and glossy. *Growth:* moderately vigorous. Liable to Black Spot.

Mme Kriloff. *H.T.* (Mcilland 1949). *Blooms:* orange yellow shaded and veined deep pink, very

Mme Louis Laperrière

large, full and of good shape. *Foliage:* plentiful and leathery. *Growth:* very vigorous and bushy.

Mme Louis Laperrière. *H.T.* (Laperrière 1952). *Blooms:* rich deep crimson, very fragrant, full and of good shape, stiff stems. *Foliage:* deep green and plentiful. *Growth:* vigorous, spreading.

Maigold. *Climber* (Kordes 1953). *Blooms:* buff yellow, large, semi-double, fragrant, profuse early and few later. *Foliage:* light green, glossy. *Growth:* very vigorous, stems thorny. (Col. pl. between pp. 56 and 57.)

Manx Queen. *Flor.* (Alex. Dickson & Sons 1963). *Blooms:* gold with orange tips, small, large

Manx Queen

open cluster, fragrant. *Foliage:* dark green. *Growth:* bushy and compact.

Ma Perkins. *Flor.* (Boerner, Jackson & Perkins 1952). *Blooms:* double, cupped, salmon, shell pink, fragrant. *Foliage:* rich green. *Growth:* vigorous and bushy.

Marcelle Gret. *H.T.* (Meilland 1947). *Blooms:* of moderate size, rich deep golden yellow. *Foliage:* dark green and glossy. *Growth:* vigorous and upright.

Märchenland. *Flor.* (Tantau 1951). *Blooms:* pale pink, deeper reverse, in large well spaced trusses,

Märchenland

semi-double, fragrant. *Foliage:* deep green, glossy. *Growth:* very vigorous and tall.

Margaret. *H.T.* (Alex. Dickson 1954). *Blooms:* soft pink with silvery reverse, very shapely and full. *Foliage:* large, deep green and plentiful. *Growth:* vigorous and moderately tall.

Margaret

Marielle. *Flor.* (De Ruiter 1964). *Blooms:* scarlet in large trusses, semi-double opening large (4 ins.). *Foliage:* dark green with coppery tints when young. *Growth:* vigorous, bushy.

Mary Wallace. *Rambler* (Van Fleet 1924). *Blooms:* very large, semi-double, fragrant, pale pink, very prolific in June, non-recurrent. *Foliage:* rich green. *Growth:* very vigorous, useful in arch, pillar or pergola.

Masquerade. *Flor.* (Boerner, Jackson & Perkins 1950). *Blooms:* yellow in bud opening to salmon pink then red, all colours on the bush at once, very free. *Foliage:* dark green. *Growth:* very vigorous, bushy.

Masquerade

McGredy's Sunset. *H.T.* (McGredy 1936). *Blooms:* deep chrome yellow, tinged with bright scarlet, on inside, and rich yellow on outside of petals, moderate sized. *Foliage:* bronze green and glossy. *Growth:* moderate, makes a good low bush.

McGredy's Yellow. *H.T.* (McGredy 1933). *Blooms:* bright yellow, large and of good shape, high centred. *Foliage:* sparse. *Growth:* quite vigorous and tall.

Mermaid

Meg. *Large-flowered Climber* (Gosset 1954). *Blooms:* apricot, shading to rich pink, semi-double, large cluster, some bloom in autumn but not strongly recurrent. *Foliage:* dark and glossy. *Growth:* quite vigorous, a good pillar rose. (Col. pl. between pp. 56 and 57.)

Memoriam. *H.T.* (Von Abrams 1960). *Blooms:* white with pale pink shading, of very good form and substance, does not like rain. *Foliage:* dark green and leathery. *Growth:* vigorous and tall.

Mermaid. *Bracteata Climber* (Paul 1917). *Blooms:* pale yellow with amber-yellow stamens, very large single blooms, fully recurrent, in fact continuous. *Foliage:* mid-green and glossy. *Growth:* very vigorous when once established but often a slow starter. No pruning, except removal of dead wood.

Message. *H.T.* (Meilland 1956). *Blooms:* pure white, of good form and substance, much better under glass as it dislikes rain. *Foliage:* light green and leathery. *Growth:* moderate, upright.

Message

Meteor

Meteor. *Flor.* (Kordes 1958). *Blooms:* vermilion red, semi-double in moderately sized trusses. *Foliage:* light green. *Growth:* uniform, short and bushy. (See plate on previous page.)

Michèle Meilland. *H.T.* (Meilland 1945). *Blooms:* salmon pink, moderately large, high centred, of good shape, fragrant. *Foliage:* bright green. *Growth:* vigorous and tall.

Milord. *H.T.* (McGredy 1962). *Blooms:* crimson scarlet, large, well formed, moderately full

Miracle

Milord

petalled, fragrant. *Foliage:* dark green. *Growth:* vigorous and upright.

Miracle. *Flor.* (G. Verbeek 1958). *Blooms:* orange salmon flushed coral, semi-double in large trusses, fragrant. *Foliage:* glossy. *Growth:* very vigorous.

Mischief. *H.T.* (McGredy 1960). *Blooms:* large, well formed, coral salmon. *Foliage:* abundant, light green. *Growth:* vigorous, bushy.

Miss Delightful. *Flor.* (Sanday 1966). *Blooms:* bright yellow in very large well spaced trusses, rosette form, fragrant. *Foliage:* bright green and glossy. *Growth:* very vigorous and tall. (Col. pl. between pp. 56 and 57.)

Miss Ireland. *H.T.* (McGredy 1960). *Blooms:* moderately full, good shape, golden orange and yellow bicolour, rather fleeting. *Foliage:* dark green. *Growth:* moderate and bushy.

Mojave. *H.T.* (Swim 1954). *Blooms:* deep orange and flame red, of moderate size and good

Mischief

form. *Foliage:* glossy and abundant. *Growth:* very vigorous and upright.

Monique. *H.T.* (Paolino 1949). *Blooms:* silvery pink with touch of salmon and yellow at base of petals, very fragrant. *Foliage:* rich green and plentiful. *Growth:* tall and upright.

Montezuma. *H.T.* (Swim 1956). *Blooms:* very large, deep salmon red, of good form and

Monique

Mrs Sam McGredy. *H.T.* (McGredy 1929). *Blooms:* bright coppery orange scarlet, of good form and substance. *Foliage:* most attractive copper beech when young, bronze green as it matures. *Growth:* moderately vigorous. The climbing sport of this variety is vigorous but

Mrs Sam McGredy

Montezuma

My Choice

substance, particularly good in autumn, dislikes rain. *Foliage:* large and handsome, bronze green. *Growth:* very vigorous, tall and branching.

Moulin Rouge. *Flor.* (Meilland 1952). *Blooms:* bright glowing scarlet in large, well and evenly spaced trusses, does not mind rain. *Foliage:* bright, mid-green, somewhat sparse. *Growth:* vigorous and upright.

blooms are apt to be restricted to the top of the branches. Both suffer from Black Spot in some areas.

My Choice. *H.T.* (Le Grice 1958). *Blooms:* pink with yellow base on the inside, pale yellow on the outside of petals, of good form and substance, high centred, very fragrant. *Foliage:* large and dark green. *Growth:* vigorous, tall and bushy. (See plate on previous page.)

Nevada. *Shrub* (Dot 1927). *Blooms:* very large, semi-double creamy white, continuing throughout the season. *Foliage:* good and plentiful. *Growth:* vigorous, making a graceful large bush.

New Dawn

Nevada

New Dawn. *Rambler* (Dreer 1930). *Blooms:* similar to Dr Van Fleet of which it is a sport, but has good recurrent bloom. *Foliage:* dark green and glossy. *Growth:* vigorous, makes a good pillar rose, 8 ft.

Nymphenburg. *Shrub* (Kordes 1954). *Blooms:* salmon pink with yellow base, in small clusters, large and semi-double. *Foliage:* large, mid-green and glossy. *Growth:* very vigorous.

Ohlala. *Flor.* (Tantau 1957). *Blooms:* crimson

scarlet with paler centre, large, semi-double, golden stamens, large trusses. *Foliage:* large, dark green, disease resistant. (Col. pl. facing p. 56.)

Opera. *H.T.* (Gaujard 1949). *Blooms:* orange red suffused with carmine, yellow at base of petals, large and shapely, fragrant. *Foliage:* light green. *Growth:* vigorous and upright.

Ophelia. *H.T.* (Paul 1912). *Blooms:* pale flesh colour, centre tinted yellow, full petalled,

Nymphenburg

Opera

may need protection from Black Spot. *Growth:* vigorous, tall and bushy.

Orange Sensation. *Flor.* (De Ruiter 1960). *Blooms:* brilliant, orange vermilion, shading to yellow at the base, in well spaced large trusses, moderately sized 2½ ins. when fully open. *Foliage:* mid-green and rather small, in some areas needs protection from Black Spot. *Growth:* vigorous and bushy. (Col. pl. facing p. 56.)

Paddy McGredy. *Flor.* (McGredy 1962). *Blooms:* hybrid-tea type in moderately sized trusses, carmine with lighter reverse, fragrant. *Foliage:* grey-green. *Growth:* dwarf and bushy.

shapely, high centred, very fragrant. *Foliage:* good. *Growth:* vigorous and tall. The climbing sport of this variety (Dickson 1920) is very vigorous and similar in all other respects to the parent.

Orangeade. *Flor.* (McGredy 1959). *Blooms:* brilliant orange vermilion, semi-double, often coming singly in early part of season, but giving large trusses later. *Foliage:* large, bronze green,

Paddy McGredy

Ophelia

Papa Meilland. *H.T.* (Alain Meilland 1963). *Blooms:* dark velvety crimson, large, double, high centred, very fragrant. *Foliage:* dark green and plentiful. *Growth:* vigorous and upright.

Paprika. *Flor.* (Tantau 1958). *Blooms:* bright Turkey red, slightly blue shading towards centre, semi-double in large well spaced trusses. *Foliage:* bronze green and large. *Growth:* vigorous and tall.

Parade. *Large-flowered Climber* (Boerner, Jackson & Perkins 1957). *Blooms:* deep rose pink shaded crimson, large, double, cupped, in small clusters, always in bloom. *Foliage:* glossy. *Growth:* very vigorous to 10 ft.

Paris Match. *H.T.* (Meilland 1956). *Blooms:* double, carmine to rose, with darker centre, well formed and high centred. *Foliage:* leathery. *Growth:* vigorous and upright.

Parkdirektor Riggers. *Kordesii Climber* (Kordes 1957). *Blooms:* velvety crimson, in very large clusters, recurrent. *Foliage:* dark green and glossy. *Growth:* vigorous, suitable for wall, fence, screen, or tall pillar.

Peace

Peace. *H.T.* (Meilland 1945). *Blooms:* vary in colour from place to place, sometimes rich deep yellow with strong shading of cerise pink on the edges of petals, sometimes pale yellow with not so strong edge colouring, very large, full petalled and of good shape, attractive when fully open. *Foliage:* large, glossy deep green. *Growth:* very vigorous, should be pruned lightly and grown as a shrub to get free flowering.

Penelope. '*Hybrid Musk*' *Shrub* (Pemberton 1924). *Blooms:* medium size, shell pink, fading to cream, with yellow centre, in large trusses, fragrant, recurrent. *Foliage:* rather small and dark green. *Growth:* bushy, makes a good hedge.

Percy Thrower. *H.T.* (Lens 1964). *Blooms:* large, double, well formed, fragrant, clear rose

Paul's Scarlet Climber

Pascali. *H.T.* (Lens 1963). *Blooms:* white, of good shape and medium size. *Foliage:* dark green. *Growth:* vigorous, compact and bushy.

Paul's Lemon Pillar. *Large-flowered Climber* (Paul 1915). *Blooms:* pale lemon yellow to cream, very large and shapely, high centred, fragrant, summer only. *Foliage:* rather small but plentiful. *Growth:* very vigorous, suitable for wall or screen.

Paul's Scarlet Climber. *Climber* (Paul 1915). *Blooms:* bright crimson, medium size, semi-double, in small clusters. *Foliage:* mid-green. *Growth:* vigorous as a pillar rose.

Penelope

Percy Thrower

pink. *Foliage:* large and glossy. *Growth:* vigorous, somewhat irregular and spreading.

Perfecta. *H.T.* (Kordes 1957). *Blooms:* large, double, very full petalled, of good shape, high centred, cream tipped, then flushed crimson,

Piccadilly

suffused with yellow, fragrant. *Foliage:* deep green and glossy. *Growth:* very upright and tall.

Piccadilly. *H.T.* (McGredy 1959). *Blooms:* moderately full, rich scarlet, shading to buttercup yellow near base of petals, pale yellow reverse, slightly fragrant. *Foliage:* attractive, bronze red in young stage and glossy olive green later. *Growth:* reasonably vigorous.

Picture. *H.T.* (McGredy 1932). *Blooms:* medium size, double, well formed, velvety, clear rose pink. *Foliage:* mid-green and adequate. *Growth:* vigorous, tall.

Pink Favourite

Pigalle. *H.T.* (Meilland 1951). *Blooms:* an unusual colour, purple crimson with buff reverse and touches of blue, large, globular, little or no fragrance. *Foliage:* bronze green. *Growth:* bushy.

Pink Favourite. *H.T.* (Von Abrams 1956). *Blooms:* deep rose-pink with pale pink at the tips when reflexed, very large, high centred, good shape, little or no fragrance. *Foliage:* rich green and very glossy. *Growth:* vigorous and tall.

Pink Parfait. *Flor.* (Swim 1962). *Blooms:* hybrid-tea type, varying shades of pink with pale orange at the base of the petals, medium sized, carried in very large trusses. *Foliage:* mid-green. *Growth:* vigorous, giving compact bush. (Col. pl. between pp. 56 and 57.)

Pink Perpetue. *Large-flowered Climber* (Gregory 1965). *Blooms:* medium size, double, globular, but when open showing quartering, fragrant, bright rose pink, in small clusters, good recurrent flowers. *Foliage:* light green. *Growth:* vigorous, good pillar 6–8 ft. (Col. pl. between pp. 56 and 57.)

Poulsen's Bedder. *Flor.* (Poulsen 1948). *Blooms:* an attractive rose-pink, large, semi-double, in big trusses. *Foliage:* bronze green. *Growth:* vigorous, upright.

Prestige. *Shrub* (Kordes 1957). *Blooms:* large, semi-double, bright scarlet in small trusses. *Foliage:* dense and dark green. *Growth:* vigorous and bushy.

Queen Elizabeth

Red Dandy. *Flor.* (Norman 1960). *Blooms:* hybrid-tea type, large, double, little or no fragrance, bright scarlet-crimson. *Foliage:* mid-green. *Growth:* vigorous and upright with branching stems.

Red Devil. *H.T.* (Alex. Dickson & Sons 1966). *Blooms:* large, full petalled, of excellent shape, high centred, good fragrance, scarlet with lighter reverse. *Foliage:* mid-green. *Growth:* very vigorous and tall.

Prima Ballerina

Prima Ballerina. *H.T.* (Tantau 1958). *Blooms:* medium sized, of good form, semi-double, very fragrant, cherry pink. *Foliage:* good, mid-green. *Growth:* very free.

Purity. *Rambler* (Hooper & Thomas 1917). *Blooms:* pure white, semi-double, fragrant, profuse summer flowering. *Foliage:* very attractive and glossy. *Growth:* vigorous, heavily thorned.

Queen Elizabeth. *Flor.* (Lammerts 1955). *Blooms:* hybrid-tea type, globular and full, rich pink, trusses small in early part of season, much larger in autumn. *Foliage:* large, rich green, leathery. *Growth:* very vigorous, upright, tall, makes a good hedge.

Red Dandy

Red Favourite

Red Favourite. *Flor.* (Tantau 1951). *Blooms:* very large trusses of rich deep crimson, semi-double, does not mind rain. *Foliage:* dark green and leathery, glossy. *Growth:* of moderate height and compact.

Ritter Von Barmstede. *Kordesii Climber* (Kordes 1960). *Blooms:* dark rose pink, double, in clusters, recurrent. *Foliage:* glossy and disease resistant. *Growth:* exceptionally vigorous, pillar up to 10 ft. or may be used as a trailer on banks.

Rose Gaujard. *H.T.* (Gaujard 1958). *Blooms:* long pointed in early stages, becoming cupped, many split, very large and full petalled, cherry red splashed with silvery white and reverse silvery white. *Foliage:* rich deep green, glossy and leathery. *Growth:* very vigorous.

Royal Highness

Rose of Tralee. *Flor.* (McGredy 1964). *Blooms:* full petalled, large when open, 4 ins., pink shaded salmon, in good trusses. *Foliage:* dark green. *Growth:* vigorous but short and bushy.

Royal Gold. *Large-flowered Climber* (Morey 1957). *Blooms:* rich deep yellow, full and of good shape, in small clusters, recurrent. *Foliage:* dark green and glossy. *Growth:* moderately vigorous, but may need protection against frost or east winds, a good pillar rose.

Royal Highness. *H.T.* (Swim 1962). *Blooms:*

Ritter Von Barmstede

light pink, high centred, and full petalled, fragrant. *Foliage:* dark green and glossy. *Growth:* upright and bushy.

Salmon Perfection. *Flor.* (De Ruiter 1951). *Blooms:* in very large trusses, salmon with orange shading, small but full and free. *Foliage:* dark green. *Growth:* vigorous and bushy.

Sanders' White. *Rambler* (Sanders 1915). *Blooms:* summer only, small, double, white, fragrant. *Foliage:* bright green. *Growth:* very vigorous, suitable for pergola, arch or pillar.

Sarah Arnot

Sarah Van Fleet. *Rugosa Shrub* (Van Fleet 1926). *Blooms:* bright rose pink in clusters, semi-double, continuous throughout the season, very fragrant. *Foliage:* typically rugosa, mid-green and leathery. *Growth:* vigorous, tall and bushy.

Scarlet Queen Elizabeth. *Flor.* (Alex. Dickson & Sons 1963). *Blooms:* globular, full petalled, orange scarlet, in moderately sized clusters. *Foliage:* bronzy green. *Growth:* vigorous, not so tall as the pink Queen Elizabeth.

Scented Air. *Flor.* (Alex. Dickson & Sons 1965). *Blooms:* hybrid-tea type, large and full

Sanders' White

Sarabande. *Flor.* (Meilland 1957). *Blooms:* in large trusses, dazzling scarlet, semi-double, always in bloom throughout season. *Foliage:* large and plentiful. *Growth:* vigorous, bushy.

Sarah Arnot. *H.T.* (Croll 1956). *Blooms:* full petalled, of good shape, high centred, fragrant, rose pink. *Foliage:* good and abundant. *Growth:* vigorous, upright.

Scarlet Queen Elizabeth

petalled, a pleasing shade of geranium lake, with edges a paler pink, very fragrant. *Foliage:* rich deep green, rather small. *Growth:* vigorous and upright.

Sea Pearl. *Flor.* (Alex. Dickson & Sons 1965). *Blooms:* hybrid-tea type, long pointed in bud, opening to shapely, high-centred blooms, pearly pink with outside of petals pink richly suffused with peach and sulphur yellow. *Foliage:* plentiful, dark green. *Growth:* moderately tall and upright.

Sea Pearl

Shepherd's Delight. *Flor. Shrub* (Alex. Dickson 1958). *Blooms:* flame, orange and yellow, brilliant in summer, paler in autumn, semi-double, in well spaced clusters, fragrant. *Foliage:* deep green with matt surface. *Growth:* very vigorous and bushy.

Shiralee. *H.T.* (Alex. Dickson & Sons 1965). *Blooms:* very large and double, high centred, saffron yellow flushed with orange. *Foliage:* an attractive green. *Growth:* vigorous and tall.

Shot Silk. *H.T.* (Alex. Dickson 1924). *Blooms:* cherry cerise shaded orange salmon, full petalled, high centred, very fragrant. *Foliage:* mid-green and glossy. *Growth:* vigorous and bushy, makes a

Shiralee

good standard. The climbing sport of this variety (Prince 1937) is very vigorous, producing a rich supply of exquisite blooms.

Silver Lining. *H.T.* (Alex. Dickson 1958). *Blooms:* of perfect form, full petalled, high centred, silvery rose with silvery reverse, dislikes rain, but excellent in autumn and in a dry summer. *Foliage:* deep green but rather sparse. *Growth:* vigorous, tall. (Col. pl. between pp. 56 and 57.)

Soldier Boy. *Large-flowered Climber* (Le Grice 1953). *Blooms:* scarlet crimson, single, recurrent. *Foliage:* mid-green. *Growth:* moderately vigorous, makes a good pillar up to 8 ft.

Spek's Yellow. *H.T.* (Verschuren 1947). *Blooms:* rich yellow, shapely, medium sized, often coming in large trusses of perfect blooms, colour does not fade in sunshine. *Foliage:* rich green and glossy, rather small. *Growth:* tall and upright.

Stella. *H.T.* (Tantau 1959). *Blooms:* large and of good form with high centres, cream flushed with pink and petals edged with carmine. *Foliage:* large, dark green. *Growth:* vigorous and bushy. (Col. pl. between pp. 56 and 57.)

Sterling Silver. *H.T.* (Fisher 1957). *Blooms:* lilac becoming silvery lilac, medium sized, double, rather short centre giving a cupped effect, very fragrant, liable to Black Spot in some areas, dislikes rain but is excellent under glass. *Foliage:* dark green, glossy. *Growth:* moderately vigorous, gives long stems under glass.

Summer Sunshine. *H.T.* (Swim 1962). *Blooms:* medium sized and not too heavily petalled, extremely decorative, high centred, fragrant, deep yellow, on long stems. *Foliage:* rich, dark green, leathery. *Growth:* upright, well branched.

Sweet Repose

Summer Sunshine

Super Star. *H.T.* (Tantau 1960). *Blooms:* pure light vermilion, startlingly brilliant, full petalled and of perfect form, last well when cut, fragrant. *Foliage:* mid-green, large and disease resistant. *Growth:* vigorous and very tall for a hybrid tea. (Col. pl. facing p. 56.)

Sutter's Gold. *H.T.* (Swim 1950). *Blooms:* in bud light orange splashed with red, but opening to pale yellow, well formed, moderately large, very fragrant. *Foliage:* deep green and leathery. *Growth:* tall, long stems. (Col. pl. between pp. 56 and 57.)

Sweet Repose. *Flor.* (De Ruiter 1956). *Blooms:* light yellow, amber, and pink, attractively formed, fragrant, in good trusses. *Foliage:* plentiful and deep green. *Growth:* very vigorous.

The Doctor. *H.T.* (Howard & Smith 1936).

Blooms: very large and well formed, high centred, bright silvery rose, very fragrant. *Foliage:* mid-green, needs protection from Black Spot in some areas. *Growth:* moderate, more vigorous in cool climates.

Uncle Walter

Vanity

Variety Club. *Flor.* (McGredy 1965). *Blooms:* hybrid-tea type in bud, full petalled, pink, suffused cream and yellow, fragrant. *Foliage:* abundant, dark green and glossy. *Growth:* vigorous and bushy.

Vera Dalton. *Flor.* (Norman 1961). *Blooms:* a delicate shade of pale rose, medium sized, moderately full petalled, little or no fragrance. *Foliage:* dark green. *Growth:* bushy and strong.

Vienna Charm. *H.T.* (Kordes 1963). *Blooms:* most attractive coppery orange, large, double and high centred, fragrant. *Foliage:* dark green. *Growth:* vigorous, rather leggy.

Violet Carson

Uncle Walter. *H.T. Shrub* (McGredy 1963). *Blooms:* scarlet with crimson shading, medium sized, full petalled, no fragrance. *Foliage:* coppery green. *Growth:* very vigorous, makes a good shrub.

Vanity. '*Hybrid Musk*' *Shrub* (Pemberton 1920). *Blooms:* large heads, single, deep pink, continuous flowering. *Foliage:* rather small, dark green. *Growth:* very vigorous.

Vera Dalton

Vilia. *Flor.* (Robinson 1958). *Blooms:* coral with yellow at base of petals, single, large trusses, very fragrant. *Foliage:* mid-green. *Growth:* vigorous and bushy.

Violet Carson. *Flor.* (McGredy 1963). *Blooms:* hybrid-tea type, large and well formed, soft peach pink with silvery reverse, fragrant. *Foliage:* good and plentiful. *Growth:* strong and bushy.

Violinista Costa. *H.T.* (Camprubi Nadal 1937). *Blooms:* orange carmine with gold shading, large, full petalled, rather loosely formed, fragrant. *Foliage:* dark green and plentiful. *Growth:* very vigorous and branching. Should be pruned hard.

Virgo. *H.T.* (Mallerin 1947). *Blooms:* white, medium sized, centre rather recessed, of good form, does not like rain. *Foliage:* dark green, rather small and sparse. *Growth:* reasonably vigorous.

Westminster

Virgo

sized, in good trusses, very fragrant. *Foliage:* large and plentiful. *Growth:* vigorous and bushy.

Wendy Cussons. *H.T.* (Gregory 1959). *Blooms:* large and of very good form, full petalled,

Vogue

Vogue. *Flor.* (Boerner, Jackson & Perkins 1949). *Blooms:* deep pink to carmine, medium

Zéphirine Drouhin

high centred, very fragrant, cerise flushed scarlet. *Foliage:* mid-green and plentiful. *Growth:* vigorous, rather uneven but bushy. (Col. pl. between pp. 56 and 57.)

Westminster. *H.T.* (Robinson 1959). *Blooms:* bi-coloured, cherry red reverse pale yellow, large, well formed, high centred, very fragrant. *Foliage:* dark green. *Growth:* vigorous.

Winifred Clarke. *H.T.* (Robinson 1965). *Blooms:* large and of good form and substance, high pointed centre, yellow fading to pale yellow. *Foliage:* mid-green and glossy. *Growth:* vigorous and branching.

Wisbech Gold. *H.T.* (McGredy 1964). *Blooms:* golden yellow edged with pink, moderately sized, cupped. *Foliage:* mid-green. *Growth:* strong and compact.

Zéphirine Drouhin. *Bourbon Climber* (Bizot 1868). *Blooms:* bright carmine pink, semi-double, medium sized, very fragrant, plentiful in summer and a few in autumn. *Foliage:* soft and light green. *Growth:* very vigorous and thornless.

Zweibrücken. *Kordesii Shrub* (Kordes 1955). *Blooms:* deep crimson in large clusters, double, recurrent. *Foliage:* dark green. *Growth:* very vigorous, makes a good shrub or may be trained as a pillar rose, 8 ft.

---

16. Recent Awards of Certificate of Merit by the Royal National Rose Society

Altissimo. *Climber* (Delbard-Chabert 1966). *Blooms:* dark red, semi-double opening flat. *Foliage:* dark green. *Growth:* strong and sturdy.

Bon Soir. *H.T.* (Alex. Dickson & Sons 1967). *Blooms:* peach pink, very full and shapely, slightly fragrant. *Foliage:* dark green, glossy. *Growth:* medium height, vigorous and upright.

Fred Loads. *Shrub* (R. Holmes 1967). *Blooms:* vermilion orange, single, fragrant. *Foliage:* light green, semi-glossy. *Growth:* vigorous, tall and upright.

Jubilant. *Flor.* (Alex. Dickson & Sons 1966). *Blooms:* salmon pink in bud, the full bloom is peach with silvery tints on the edges of the petals; of medium size and slightly fragrant. *Foliage* green with bronze shading. *Growth:* vigorous, tall and upright.

King Arthur. *Flor.* (R. Harkness & Co. 1967). *Blooms:* hybrid-tea type, salmon pink, large, double. *Foliage:* medium green, large. *Growth:* medium height and branching.

Red Gold. *Flor.* (Alex. Dickson & Sons 1967). *Blooms:* hybrid-tea type, golden yellow with cherry edging. *Foliage:* medium green, small, plentiful. *Growth:* vigorous, of medium height.

Travesti. *Flor.* (De Ruiter 1967). *Blooms:* yellow, with inner side of petals flushed cherry. *Foliage:* dark green, small. *Growth:* vigorous.

Index

(See page 48 for the alphabetical list of selected roses which includes a brief description of each variety.)